THE COMPLETE NUCLEAR SURVIVAL GUIDE

Tom Linden

Copyright © 2017 Tom Linden

All rights reserved

ISBN-13:978-1985059610
ISBN-10: 1985059614

Copyright © All rights reserved worldwide. No part of this document may be reproduced, stored, transmitted by any means, for profit or gain, without the expressed permission of the author.

This is not an exhaustive collection of information. All information is true and correct to the best of the Author's knowledge. The Author assumes no liability for inaccuracies or failures of equipment.

No techniques are recommended without proper safety measures and training. The author nor publisher assumes no liability for your actions.

Contents

About the Author 2

Foreword 4

The First Nuclear War 4

Civil Defence Training & Informative Films 7

COLD WAR: Underground Nuclear Monitoring 8

How to Fight a Nuclear War 11

Understanding the Terminology 13

Characteristics of Nuclear Explosions 16

Improvised Nuclear Devices (INDs) 27

Down winders 28

Radiation Reaches Alarming levels in Britain 32

The effects of EMP 35

The MOAB 39

Fears Verses Facts 41

Civil Defence 43

Civil Defence Planning Today 44

The National Attack Warning System 47

The Complete Nuclear Survival Guide

Today's Nuclear Bunkers...50

Protection 61

Fallout Room and Inner Refuge 64

Action at Attack Warning...69

Action at fallout Warnings 71

Checklists 72

Ventilation 75

Biological Effects of Nuclear Weapons 77

Health and Hygiene...79

Water 85

Reducing the risk of Fire 96

Post Attack Food Supply 97

Living off the Land..99

Storage Times for Survival foods 102

Storage Times for Tinned Foods 105

A 'modern' two week food supply...108

Home Made Faraday Cage..122

Entertainment..125

Nuclear Survival Check List 130

Detection equipment..134

N.B.C. Clothing 137

Afterword 146

BOOK TABLES 1

THE COMPLETE NUCLEAR SURVIVAL GUIDE

About the Author

I was an N.C.O. Instructor with the Royal Observer Corps for 12 years specialising in the Effects of Nuclear Weapons.

I was given an exemption from the entry exam due to my level of experience and became a member of the Institute of Civil defence giving me the appellation M.I.C.D. I remained a member between 1987 and 1992.

I was for 4 years at North Yorkshire County Council Community Defence Adviser and helped to provide the countries first ever emergency survey of a town to provide an action plan for that community, that town was Harrogate.

I also ran my own survival school in North Yorkshire in the 80's as well as a survival club for local kids.

I suspect that there are many of you who would wish to be able to protect their families should our enemies decide to explode a 'dirty bomb' on British soil for example.

We would I believe be extremely foolish to discount the potential for another Chernobyl or a Fukushima type incident to occur affecting us here in the UK, Or to suffer our very own British nuclear accident as our nuclear plants grow ever older. This is not forgetting the dangers posed by the, now developed, long range nuclear weapons held by Iran and Syria, both of which I consider to be rogue states.

This Complete Nuclear Survival Guide is just that, a guide to your survival and that of your family. Experiencing a nuclear event is almost impossible for us to contemplate for obvious reasons, as it would be the end of the world. But would it?

We as a world have had hundreds of nuclear test explosions and we are still here, the world has not ended, life goes on does it not? The question is if you survived the initial effects of a nuclear explosion, would you have the knowledge and the skills to survive the residual effects?

That is where my Complete Nuclear Survival Guide comes in, by keeping it with you in your bug-out-bag, you will not only know where to find it, but if you bug-out, so along goes this valuable survival information. Although as you will read later, I recommend bugging-in.

Foreword

The aim of this Nuclear Survival Manual is to provide you, the reader, with advice and information to help you and your family survive what would be the worst catastrophe in history… a Nuclear War. Whether it is a limited strike or an all-out strategic exchange, or a terrorist "Dirty Bomb" type attack on our country or even a Chernobyl style nuclear accident on our soil or that of an upwind neighbouring country, there will be survivors, more through good luck than good planning I would suggest.

Surviving in a nuclear environment means just another set of rules and skills we must learn.

While I was writing this manual a friend came round to visit me and said 'How could anyone survive? If the bomb dropped, we'd all be dead'. Nonsense, how would we all be dead? Where did the bomb drop? Was it ground or air burst? What size was it? Which way was the wind blowing and at what speed etc., etc., etc.

I gave him the only example I could think of. I said that if a grenade exploded in this room now, we'd be killed, but the people living 200 yards up the road would not, as the effects of the explosion are confined to a relatively small area.

The same rule, although on a much larger scale applies to nuclear explosions and if you know the facts you can calculate the effects.

A nuclear explosion is similar to any other initial chemical explosion in that it produces heat, light and a blast. However, unlike the people 200 yards up the road, if you survive the heat, light and blast (the initial effects) you will have to survive the nuclear radiation and I will show you how in this manual.

Whether you discount a nuclear war or not, you would be very foolish in my opinion to discount a nuclear attack by terrorists or a rogue nuclear state or God forbid that it should ever happen, a British Chernobyl.

The First Nuclear War

The atomic bombings of the cities of Hiroshima and Nagasaki in Japan were conducted by the United States during the final stages of World War II in 1945. These two events are the only use of nuclear weapons in war to date.

Following a firebombing campaign that destroyed many Japanese cities, the Allies prepared for a costly invasion of Japan. The war in Europe ended when Nazi Germany signed its instrument of surrender on 8 May, but the Pacific War continued.

Together with the United Kingdom and the Republic of China, the United States called for a surrender of Japan in the Potsdam Declaration on 26 July 1945, threatening Japan with "prompt and utter destruction".

The Japanese government ignored this ultimatum, and the United States deployed two nuclear weapons developed by the Manhattan Project. American airmen dropped Little Boy on the city of Hiroshima on 6 August 1945, followed by Fat Man over Nagasaki on 9 August.

Within the first two to four months of the bombings, the acute effects killed 90,000–166,000 people in Hiroshima and 60,000–80,000 in Nagasaki, with roughly half of the deaths in each city occurring on the first day.

The Hiroshima prefecture health department estimated that, of the people who died on the day of the explosion, 60% died from flash or flame burns, 30% from falling debris and 10% from other causes.

During the following months, large numbers died from the effect of burns, radiation sickness, and other injuries, compounded by illness. In a US estimate of the total immediate and short-term cause of death, 15–20% died from radiation sickness, 20–30% from burns, and 50–60% from other injuries, compounded by illness. In both cities, most of the dead were civilians, although Hiroshima had a sizable garrison.

Most of what is known about the effects of nuclear weapons on humans comes from the two atomic bombs dropped on the Japanese cities of Hiroshima and Nagasaki in 1945. There is also a lot of information from atmospheric nuclear testing and nuclear accidents. Although there are several types of nuclear weapon with varying amounts of explosive power, the effects would be the same – except on a different scale.

For example, the bomb that was exploded above Hiroshima was 15 kilotons (that's the equivalent of 15,000 tons of TNT). The Nagasaki bomb was around 21 kilotons. A single

Trident warhead is 100 kilotons. Britain has 180 of these warheads.

Note: Our methods of building construction vary tremendously from those used in 1945 in these two Japanese cities, and therefore afford us greater protection and much higher Protective factors. That, combined with prepping today, the casualty figures shown above would be a lot lower should a similar device be detonated above a British city.

Civil Defence Training & Informative Films

Film Threads "A nuclear attack on Sheffield"

http://www.youtube.com/watch?v=_MCbTvoNrAg

Film "The Day After" An attack on the USA

http://www.youtube.com/watch?v=r2B7sdLPMfc&playnext=1&list=PLfeoMaLoMTiP78MO4hrJPkYgLsCBJIAa4&feature=results_video

Film/Cartoon Civil defence training film "When the wind blows"]

http://www.youtube.com/watch?v=N9aHT-IlkHo

COLD WAR: Underground Nuclear Monitoring

With the start of the cold war and the increasing threat of nuclear attack in the 1950's, the Royal Observer Corps was given an added responsibility of reporting nuclear bursts and monitoring fall-out. This necessitated the construction of 1563 underground monitoring posts throughout Great Britain & Northern Ireland. The posts were later reduced in number to approximately 850 from 1968

It would now be necessary for these posts (as well as centres) to be occupied for at least seven days after any nuclear event, Centres were expanded with increased accommodation. Emergency power generation, air handling and filtration, and underground posts were constructed with concrete under a 200 mm slab, they were 4.75 metres long and 2.25 metres in length and height.

Altogether more sophisticated than its WW2 role; the ROC formed part of the United Kingdom Warning and Monitoring Organisation (UKWMO), which was the only organisation in Britain equipped and trained to report on radioactive fall-out on a national basis.

The fact that the Corps was trained to obtain and disseminate this information might have well meant the difference between life and death for many of us.

Initially, communications were by telephone, replaced in 1964 by Tele-talk units; these used landlines. The vulnerability of land lines lead to VHF radio being installed with one post in each cluster; clusters had local arrangements for communication between themselves.

"The Science Bit"

If nuclear weapons are used on a large scale, those of us living in the country areas might be exposed to as great a risk as those in the towns.

Following a nuclear bomb-burst, dust and debris are sucked up into the atmosphere by the explosion. After being dispersed by any subsequent wind, it falls across the country as radioactive particles also commonly known as fall-out.

The radioactive dust, falling where the wind blows it, will bring the most widespread dangers. No part of the United Kingdom could be considered safe from both the direct effects of the weapons and the resulting fallout.

Thanks to the array of instruments and apparatus embodied in the 25 reinforced Group Controls and the underground monitoring posts, the Corps would have been able to supply essential data on the arrival and intensity of the fall-out. This would enable the officers of the United Kingdom

Warning and Monitoring Organisation to advise people in the path of radioactive fallout to take cover.

The ROC was ideally suited for its role of reporting fall-out. The strategically placed network extended from the Orkneys to the far south-west. Each Group Control was in contact with a network of about 30 small monitoring posts spaced some 10 to 15 miles apart. However, although the role of the Corps had changed completely during the late 1960's / Early 1970's, the traditional links with the Royal Air Force remained. The skill of visual aircraft recognition was still maintained by post observers up until stand-down in 1991.

We no longer have the ROC and are now left to fend for ourselves without any monitoring organisation to provide us with the critical Radioactive Fallout levels that we need to plan our time in an outside environment.

So unless you have the money to purchase your own detection equipment you must plan to stay in your inner refuge until the radio announcement says it is safe to venture out and for how long.

How to Fight a Nuclear War

Revealed: Jimmy Carter's strategy for Armageddon (And it is still being used today)

Presidential Decision Directive 59 -- presented on Foreign Policy's National Security channel and on the National Security Archive's website for the first time. -- Was one of the most controversial nuclear policy documents of the Cold War, yet until now it's never been made public in its entirety.

Signed by President Jimmy Carter on July 25, 1980, the directive (titled "Nuclear Weapons Employment Policy") aimed to give presidents more flexibility in planning for and executing a nuclear war -- that is, options beyond a massive strike. Leaks of the document's Top Secret contents, within weeks of its approval, gave rise to front-page stories in the New York Times and the Washington Post, alleging that its changes to U.S. strategy lowered the threshold of a decision to go nuclear.

With other recently declassified material, PD-59 shows that the United States was indeed preparing to fight a nuclear war, with the hope of enduring. To do this, it sought a nuclear force posture that ensured a "high degree of flexibility, enduring survivability, and adequate performance in the face of enemy actions." If deterrence failed, the United States "must be capable of fighting successfully so that the adversary would not achieve his war aims and would suffer costs that are unacceptable."

Perhaps even more remarkable than this guidance is the fact that, although the Obama administration is conducting a review of U.S. nuclear targeting guidance, key concepts behind PD-59 still drive U.S. policy to this day.

The National Security Archive obtained the virtual unexpurgated document in response to a mandatory declassification review request to the Jimmy Carter Library. Highly classified for years, PD-59 was signed during a period of heightened Cold War tensions owing to the Soviet invasion of Afghanistan, greater instability in the Middle East, and earlier strains over China policy, human rights, the Horn of Africa, and Euro missiles.

Press coverage at the time elicited debate inside and outside the government, with some arguing that the directive would aggravate Cold War tensions by increasing Soviet fears about vulnerability and raising pressures for launch-on-warning in a crisis.

A key element of PD-59 was to use high-tech intelligence to find nuclear weapons targets in battlefield situations, strike the targets, and then assess the damage -- a "look-shoot-look" capability.

A memorandum from NSC military aide William Odom depicted Secretary of Defence Harold Brown doing exactly that in a recent military exercise where he was "chasing [enemy] general purpose forces in Eastern Europe and Korea with strategic weapons."

That is, he was planning how to use large nuclear weapons to defeat conventional troops. The drafters of PD-59 like Odom did not believe that deploying weapons in this way would necessarily result in apocalypse -- they believed they could control escalation during a nuclear war.

Understanding the Terminology

Firstly, let's look at some of the commonly used words and phrases used in connection with nuclear weapons and nuclear explosions.

1. Ground Zero: The point directly below the explosion
2. Yield: The power released in a nuclear explosion is expressed in terms of the total energy released as compared with T.N.T. The words Kiloton and Megaton are used to describe the size. A Kiloton is equivalent to 1,000 tons of T.N.T., the Megaton is equivalent 1,000,000 tons of T.N.T. A 500,000 Kiloton weapon is known as a ½ a Megaton. KT= Kiloton MT= Megaton.
3. Fireball: The fireball is formed at the time of the explosion. It is highly radioactive and contains extremely hot gases. Depending on the size of the weapon, the fireball can rise to 20 miles or more.

4. Initial Radiation: Is classed as all radiation released within one minute of detonation.
5. Residual Radiation: Produced from radioactive fission products and other contents of the bomb, vaporized in the intense heat of the fireball. They then condense on the dust and debris sucked up and these particles fall to earth as radioactive fallout.
6. Electromagnetic Pulse: (EMP) also known as NEMP, generally only associated with extremely bursts in excess of 2 miles. The effects of EMP can cause widespread damage to electrical equipment and all modern communication equipment unless otherwise protected.
7. Air Burst: This is where the fireball or no appreciable part of the fireball touches the ground.
8. Ground Burst: This is where the fireball or an appreciable part of the fireball does touch the ground.
9. Protective Factor: This is the factor by which the dose received by a person in a building is reduced compared with that of a person in the open. For example a protective factor of 200 means that the dose rate is 1/200of the dose rate outside.
10. Shielding: As gamma radiation passes through material, it loses its intensity. The thicker and denser the material the greater the loss.
11. Half Value Thickness: This is the thickness of material to reduce the dose rate by half.
12. Dose: The exposure dose relates to that received by a person.

13. Dose rate: The intensity of radiation at any moment in the air.
14. Roentgen or (r): Radiation measurement of exposure dose – ionised radiation in the air.
15. Roentgens per Hour (rph): Radiation measurement of the dose rate at any moment in the air.
16. RAD: Radiation measurement for our purposes equivalent to the Roentgen.
17. Alpha Particles: Nuclear radiation - effective range 5cm in the air.
18. Beta Particles: Nuclear radiation – effective range 2-3 metres in the air.
19. Gamma Particles: Nuclear radiation – effective range hundreds of feet in the air.
20. (INDs) Improvised Nuclear Devices.

Characteristics of Nuclear Explosions

The energy distribution in a nuclear explosion at or near ground level is split up as below

45% as Blast and Shock Waves

35% as Light and Heat radiation – thermal radiation

5% as Initial nuclear radiation

15% as Residual Nuclear Radiation from fission products

Light

In the instance a nuclear explosion occurs, an intense, blinding light occurs which is brighter that the sun, and lasts a number of seconds. The duration depends on the yield or the size of the weapon. Looking at the flash can cause temporary or even permanent blindness. The effect of the flash will be greater at night or in clear weather conditions.

Heat

At the moment of the explosion a large fireball is created, its size can vary from a few hundred feet to several miles in diameter depending on weapon size (see tables 1, 2, 3). The fireball is as hot as the sun, that is to say several million degrees.

Lasting some 1 to 20 seconds is a heat pulse that travels at the speed of light in straight lines away from the explosion. The heat pulse can cause severe injury to people unprotected in the open at a considerable distance from Ground Zero. For example, a 20MT could cause heat damage up to 15 miles if a ground burst and up to 25 miles if air burst.

Protective measures such as whitewashing windows, wearing light colours which reflect heat, taking cover and looking away will all help to reduce casualties considerably See (Fig. 1) (Fig 2) and (Fig 3).

Fire Zone of Ground Burst Weapons in Miles

The Power of the Weapon

Fig.1

Visibility	20KT	100KT	1/2MT	1MT	2MT	5MT	10MT	20MT
2 Miles	To 3/4	To1.1/2	To2.1/2	To3	To 2-4	To 5	To 5.1/2	6.1/2
8 Miles	To 7/8th	To 1.3/4	To 3	To 4	To 5	To 7	To 9	To 10
32 Miles	To 1	To 2	To 3.1/2	To 4	To 5	To 7	To 9	To 10

Fire Zone of Air Burst Weapons in Miles

Power of the Weapon

Fig.2

Visibility	20KT	100KT	½MT	1MT	2MT	5MT	10MT	20MT
2 Miles	To I.1/4	To 2.1/4	To 4	To 5	To 7	To 8.1/2	To 10	To 12
8 Miles	To 1.3/8	To 2.1/2	To 5	To 6.1/2	To 8	To 12	To 15	To 17
32 Miles	To 1.5/8	To 3	To 6	To 8	To 11	To 15	To 20	To 25

Heat Wave- Thermal Radiation

Power of the Weapon

Fig.3

Effect on Skin	20KT	100KT	1/2MT	1MT	2MT	5MT	10MT	20MT
Charring	1	2	4	5	6.3/4	9.1/4	12	16
Blisters	1.1/2	1.1/4	4.3/4	6.1/4	8.1/4	12	16	20
Reddening	1.3/4	3.3/4	6.1/2	8.1/2	11	16	20	25

The range in miles at which people standing in the open will be affected by differing degrees of skin burns from round burst weapons of different power.

NB. With an air burst in clear conditions, the distance could be 50% greater.

Blast

This has the longest ranging initial effect of the explosion. As it travels at the speed of sound it follows the ground contours and it is deflected by natural features. If the weapon is ground burst then a large crater is formed (See table 4). As it is formed, ground shock waves are produced rather like a mini earthquake. This will damage underground structures as well as Gas, water, electric, communication piping and cabling. Another major problem is caused by debris blocking roads etc.

Combined with this blast wave are high winds up to 300 miles per hour, which will cause injuries in two ways. Firstly, people unprotected in the open will be blown into static objects like buildings and trees and secondly, causing a greater number of casualties will be missiles hurled around by this wind. Varying items from cars, to bricks, stones, tiles and glass. Likely injuries range from broken limbs to wounding by sharp objects see (fig. 5)

Crater Size in Feet for a Ground Burst Weapon on Saturated Clay

Fig.4

Power of the Weapon

	20 KT	100KT	1/2 MT	1MT	2MT	5MT	10MT	20MT
Crater Radius A	300	510	850	1100	1360	1700	2200	2800
Crater Lip Radius A	600	1020	1700	2200	2700	3400	4400	5600
Crater Depth B	40	55	80	100	120	150	180	210

(A) To get ranges (radii) in dry soil, divide by 1.7

(B) To get depths in dry soil divide by 0.7

(A) To get ranges (radii) in hard rock divide by 2

(B) To get depths in hard rock divide by 0.9

Radiation

When a nuclear explosion occurs, several types of radiation are produced they are Alpha, Beta, Gamma and even X-rays and neutrons. Without the use of specialised measuring equipment, you will not detect nuclear radiation and you certainly cannot hear, see or smell it. Nuclear radiation is harmful to living organisms and occurs in two stages initial and residual. (See Fig 6).

Distance in miles of the effect on people in the open, exposed to initial Gamma radiation

Air burst or ground Burst

Power of the Weapon

Fig.6

	20KT	100KT	.5 MT	1MT	2MT	5MT	10MT	20MT
50% survival for 450r	3/4	1	1.1/4	1.1/2	1.3/4	2	2.1/4	2.1/4
NO appreciable risk of sickness 75r	1	1.1/4	1.1/2	1.3/4	2	2.1/4	2.1/2	2.1/2

Initial Radiation

Depending on the size of the weapon the rate of radiation varies, but most is received in the first few seconds whilst the fireball is closest to the ground (e.g. 90% of the total dose from a 10KT weapon is received within 5 seconds). This radiation consists of neutrons and gamma rays and both cause damage to the living cells of the human body, but would not be the main cause of fatalities from a large weapon as anyone close enough to the explosion to receive a lethal dose would certainly be killed by the effects of the heat and blast first.

Residual Radiation

This is produced by a ground burst weapon from the earth removed from the large crater formed by the explosion as the fireball rises, thousands of tons of earth, rock, stone, etc. is sucked up into the air and can reach heights of 20 miles or more depending on the size of the weapon. As the mushroom shaped cloud stabilises and cools the sucked up particles which have become highly radioactive start to fall back to earth as radioactive fallout; the large heavier particles falling closer to GZ while the lighter particles are carried downwind hundreds of miles depositing radioactive fallout as they travel thus providing the biggest radiation hazard to the population or populations of other countries (See Fig. 7 and Fig.8).

Fall-out dust carried by winds over a wide area and can even be talcum powder size.

Fig.7

Continental Fallout can affect the UK

Fig.8

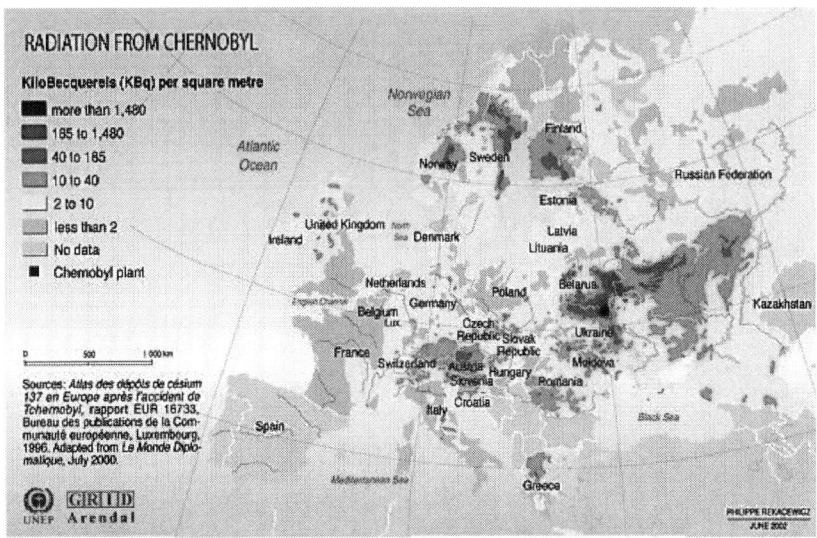

Summary of Effects

Light: Immediate, brighter than the sun and lasts for several seconds.

Heat: Immediate, lasts 1 to 20 seconds and travels in straight lines at the speed of light, one of the main casualty producing effects of nuclear explosions.

Initial radiation: Follows in 1 second of commencement of the light flash. It is produced by the weapon within one minute of the explosion.

Blast: Follows from about half a second to several seconds after light and heat flash. It travels at the speed of sound and has the longest range of the immediate causality producing effects.

Fires: They may be ignited by the heat flash but would be either extinguished or increased by the wind from the blast wave.

Fallout: Between 30 minutes and several hours after a blast fallout starts to arrive. It all depends on the wind speed and direction. Fallout only occurs with a ground burst. Radiation from fallout decreases by a factor of 10 for each 7-fold increase in time. (E.g. The Seven tenths rule).

So as you can see if the fireball does not touch the ground, no crater is formed. So there is no debris to be carried up into the fireball, which means that no radioactive fallout can occur. Although no "air burst" weapon as we have seen causes radioactive fallout or a long-term radiation hazard, an air burst does cause greater blast damage over a much wider area, but its effects are confined to heat, light, blast, EMP and initial radiation – all lasting only minutes.

Improvised Nuclear Devices (INDs)

An illicit nuclear weapon bought, stolen, or otherwise originating from a nuclear state, or a weapon fabricated by a terrorist group from illegally obtained fissile nuclear weapons material that produces a nuclear explosion

Built from the components of a stolen weapon or from scratch using nuclear material, (plutonium or highly enriched uranium) produces the same physical and medical effects as a nuclear weapon explosion. It results in catastrophic loss of life, destruction of infrastructure, and contamination of a very large area

If nuclear yield is NOT achieved, the result would likely resemble a Radiological Dispersal Device in which fissile weapons material was dispensed locally. The main effect would be the denial of the area to those who once lived and worked there for some considerable time.

There would also be a danger from downwind radioactive particles dispersal e.g. radioactive fallout, although it may be of a very low yield, until monitored and measured it should be treated as high level fallout and you should retreat to your fallout room.

If nuclear yield is achieved, the results would resemble a nuclear explosion and must be treated as such.

Down winders

Down winders refers to individuals and communities who are exposed to radioactive contamination or nuclear fallout from atmospheric or underground nuclear weapons testing, and nuclear accidents. Here I focus on incidents in the United States, or those caused by its weapons testing.

More generally, the term can also include those communities and individuals who are exposed to ionizing radiation and other emissions due to the regular production and maintenance of nuclear weapons, nuclear power, and nuclear waste. Down winders may be exposed to releases of radioactive materials into the environment that contaminate their groundwater systems, food chains, and the air they breathe. Some down winders may have suffered acute exposure due to their involvement in uranium mining and nuclear experimentation.

Several severe adverse health effects, such as an increased incidence of cancers, non-cancerous thyroid diseases, and congenital malformations have been observed in many and diverse "downwind" communities exposed to nuclear fallout and radioactive contamination.

The impact of nuclear contamination on an individual is generally estimated as the result of the dose of radiation received and the duration of exposure, using the Linear No-Threshold Model (LNT). Sex, age, race, culture, occupation, class, location, and simultaneous exposure to additional environmental toxins are also significant, but often overlooked, factors that contribute to the health effects on a particular "downwind" community.

Between 1945 and 1980, the United States, U.S.S.R, United Kingdom, France and China exploded 504 nuclear devices in atmospheric tests at thirteen primary sites yielding the explosive equivalent of 440 megatons of TNT. Of these atmospheric tests, 330 were conducted by the United States.

Accounting for all types of nuclear tests, official counts show that the United States has conducted 1,054 nuclear weapons tests to date, involving at least 1,151 nuclear devices, most of which occurred at Nevada Test Site and the Pacific Proving Grounds in the Marshall Islands, with ten other tests taking place at various locations in the United States, including Alaska, Colorado, Mississippi, and New Mexico.

There have been an estimated 2,000 nuclear tests conducted worldwide; the number of nuclear tests conducted by the United States alone is currently more than the sum of nuclear testing done by all other known nuclear states (USSR, Great Britain, France, China, India, Pakistan, North Korea) combined.

These nuclear tests infused vast quantities of radioactive material into the world's atmosphere, which was widely dispersed and then deposited as global fallout.

The nuclear explosions produce a characteristic mushroom cloud, which moves downwind as it reaches its stabilization height. Dispersion of the radioactive elements causes vertical and lateral cloud movement, spreading radioactive materials over adjacent regions.

While larger particles settle nearby the site of the detonation, smaller particles and gases may be dispersed around the world. Additionally, some explosions injected radioactive material into the stratosphere, more than 10 kilometres above ground-level, meaning it may float there for years before being subsequently deposited uniformly around the earth. Global fallout is the result, which exposes everything to an elevated level of man-made background radiation.

While "down winders" refers to those who live and work closest to the explosion site and are thus most acutely affected, there is a global effect of increased health risks due to ionizing radiation in the atmosphere.

The earliest concerns raised about the health effects of exposure to nuclear fallout had to do with fears of genetic alterations that may occur among the offspring of those most exposed. However, the observed inheritable effects of radiation exposure, by groups with histories of acute risk, are considered minimal. Compared with the significant increase in thyroid cancer, leukaemia and certain solid tumours that have developed within a decade or more after exposure.

As studies of biological samples (including bone, thyroid glands and other tissues) have been undertaken, it has become increasingly clear that specific radionuclides in fallout are implicated in fallout-related cancers and other late effects.

In 1980, People magazine revealed some consequences of continental nuclear testing for American citizens. The magazine disclosed that of some 220 cast and crew who filmed a 1956 film, The Conqueror, on location near St. George, Utah, ninety-one had come down with cancer, with an unheard of 41 percent morbidity rate. Of these, forty-six had died of cancer by 1980. Among the victims were John Wayne and Susan Hayward, the stars of the film.

Radiation Reaches Alarming levels in Britain

Maybe all the people that live within an area from Birmingham across to Norwich and down to Bristol, Bournemouth and across to Dover and back up to Norwich were not aware that they may have been exposed, on more than one occasion, extremely high levels of radiation from the weapons used by the US, UK and coalition forces in and around the Middle East war zones……not to mention the onslaught on Libya that saw an incredible amount of DU weapons being used and also possibly low yield nuclear weapons.

Back in the 1940's during the Los Alamos nuclear test they discovered a type of poisonous gaseous substance that was emitted from the weapons. The Generals seized this new found substance as a potential people killer that basically would drift on the wind, have no footprint to identify the aggressor and would kill over a long period of time.

A secret memo to Brigadier General Grove clearly showed their intention to carry out mass genocide, mass depopulation and mass infertility using this technology resulting in the development of depleted uranium (DU) weapons as used extensively today in all areas of conflict. If you don't believe me ask the people of Iraq, especially those living in Fallujah and Basra who may not to be able to ever have a child.

It was in more recent times they seized an opportunity to dispose of the nuclear waste from their nuclear programmes (Uranium 238 or DU) as existing stockpiles were massive and in very poor condition and so it made sense to give it away to the arms manufacturing companies to be used as a penetrator, shaped charged liner or simply for ballast in weapons and aircraft etc.

DU is pyrophoric which basically means it is self-igniting at low temperatures around 170 degrees. When it leaves the barrel of a gun it is basically igniting, like tracer bullets. Upon hitting the target it erupts into a massive thermonuclear type explosion in access of 5000 degrees and emits a huge cloud of radioactive nano-particles in their millions that then drift on the wind.

When one breaths in the nano-particles from DU it's extremely easy to become ill with many forms of cancer, especially the unborn fetus and children. One expert stated that breathing in just ten milligrams of uranium oxide dust would exceed any safe limit.

From my perspective there is no safe limit of radiation and certainly no one has studied the impact of breathing in DU. A Dr. Jack Valentin, stated "If you were actually inside, or immediately outside, the vehicle that's hit by a bullet, and if you survive that hit, you can imagine that person inhaling perhaps a hundred milligrams."

My comment would therefore be if this is the case with a single bullet imagine the consequences of shells, bombs and cruise missiles that are fired off each and every day that contain thousands of kilograms.

DU evidence simply lies around after every conflict i.e. the Balkans, Kuwait, Iraq, Afghanistan, North Pakistan, Lebanon, Gaza, Yemen, Somalia and now Libya. Its detected in damaged tanks, vehicles, spent rounds sitting on the surface, buildings, or simply in the soil.

These deadly nano-particles are not only circling the countries of conflict but also adjacent countries and the world. Its half-life is 4.5 billion years, every time it rains or snows it comes down to contaminate our soil, crops and water and continues to be stirred up by the weather, gales, sand storms which stretch across continents. Every time we drive or walk on it secondary contamination occurs.

The effects of EMP

Identifying the systems that would probably fail if there were a strong-enough EMP from either a massive solar CME, a nuclear EMP weapon, or a tactical EMP bomb, is easier to speculate than items that might survive an EMP. There are some obvious items that would survive, but many are not that obvious.

An EMP, an 'electro-magnetic-pulse', is a side-effect of a nuclear explosion, a coronal mass ejection (from the Sun), or a purposed EMP bomb. An EMP is a near instantaneous and invisible 'ZAP' of electricity that surges through electrical wires and electrical semiconductor components.

'IF' the EMP is strong enough and the electronic components are close enough to the source, then these components could fry. Once they are fried, that's it…they're done. Only physical replacements will bring the systems back up and running.

So, while attempting to discover what items will survive an EMP, we need to know what is INSIDE the item… namely, if there are any electronic semiconductors (transistors, IC 'chips', microprocessors, etc.).

It is the microscopic semiconductor 'junctions' themselves that are vulnerable to melting due to an excess of electrical current being forced through the junction (from the EMP).

Also, an EMP will be carried through overhead power lines (at the speed of light) and could instantaneously overwhelm power transformers along the grid with excess electrical current, causing the windings of the transformers to melt into a molten blob. The power lines will also carry the EMP (at the speed of light) far and wide into homes and businesses in search of semiconductors to fry.

Here's another thing you need to know… an EMP's energy will decay the further away from the source that you get. Electronic circuits that are further away will be less vulnerable to the EMP. How far away? Well that depends (of course). It depends on the overall strength of the EMP, the altitude of the EMP, the 'line-of-sight' distance from the EMP, and any protection that the device might have to protect it from an EMP.

After all that, the simple answer to what items might survive, are those items that do not contain semiconductors!

The problem is, nearly all devices today contain semiconductors!

If the device you are wondering about contains any digital interface whatsoever, then you can probably kiss it good-bye. Often it may be difficult to even know if there are semiconductors in a device. Even if there is no digital interface, there could still very well be semiconductors or electronic circuits somewhere inside.

Electric heaters... Forget about it. The grid will probably be down.

Oil heat... The burner's ignition transformers, electronic control circuits, and electronic controlled pumps will fry. Plus, with no electrical power, the pumps won't function.

Natural gas heat... The utility gas pressure will probably remain for a while, but electronic thermostats or gas valve controllers may fry. Some basic-style natural gas heaters, such as wall units, could be lit manually though – until the pressure runs out.

Portable heaters... Most self-fueled heaters without electronic controls will survive –until your fuel source runs out. If it plugs in, it's toast.

Wood Stove heater... Ding, Ding, Ding... we have a winner!

Now let's talk cars.

As most of us know, any new car today is jam packed full of electronics. Forget it. It's dead.

Any car made with electronic ignition and fuel injection will probably stop in its tracks.

Cars have been being built with these features longer than you may think in fact since the (1980's). Depending on the exact vehicle, you may be somewhat 'safe' with a car built in the early 1980's, 1970's or earlier.

It would take some significant research to list the vehicles built without these electronic systems but suffice it to say that most any vehicle today is vulnerable to EMP failure (if close enough to the EMP source). So should you re-think your choice of bug out vehicle?

Let's talk in general terms.

Generally speaking, ranging from tools, to appliances, to heaters, to vehicles… if it has electronic circuits, it is vulnerable to EMP. This basically leaves hand tools, hand operated or primitive appliances, wood stove heat, and old vehicles. We're talking living like the 1800's or earlier.

While the threat of an EMP to the degree of mass power cuts is apparently slim, the fact is that it is not zero.

A huge portion of the world population today relies on electricity for survival. It has enabled great advancements in civilization. The lack thereof could enable great setbacks to civilization.

So be prepared!!

The MOAB

I thought that I would include information on this American bomb, here are the basic facts about the MOAB:

It is currently the largest conventional bomb (as opposed to a nuclear bomb) in the U.S. arsenal.

The bomb weighs 21,000 pounds (9,525 kg).

The bomb is 30 feet long and 40.5 inches in diameter.

It is satellite-guided, making it a very large "smart bomb."

It bursts about 6 feet (1.8 meters) above the ground.

The idea behind an "air burst" weapon, as opposed to a weapon that explodes on impact with the ground, is to increase its destructive range. A bomb that penetrates the ground and then bursts tends to send all of its energy either down into the ground or straight up into the air. An air burst weapon sends a great deal of its energy out to the side.

The MOAB will replace the BLU-82, also known as the Daisy Cutter, a 15,000-pound (6,800-kg) air-burst bomb developed during the Vietnam War. The Air Force could drop a Daisy Cutter to create an instant helicopter landing site. The explosive force would clear out trees in a 500-foot-diameter (152-meter) circle.

The MOAB is not the largest bomb ever created. In the 1950s the United States manufactured the T-12, a 43,600-pound (19,800-kg) bomb that could be dropped from the B-36.

Compared to a nuclear bomb, the MOAB produces a tiny explosion. The smallest known nuclear bomb -- the Davy Crockett fission bomb -- has a 10-ton yield. The difference is that a nuclear bomb that small, weighs less than 100 pounds (45 kg) and produces significant amounts of lethal radiation when it detonates. In comparison, the nuclear bomb dropped on Hiroshima had a yield of 14,500 tons of TNT and weighed only 10,000 pounds (4,500 kg) -- half the weight of the MOAB.

Fears Verses Facts

Fear

If a nuclear war or a nuclear terrorist attack occurred the radioactive fallout would poison the air and every part of the environment and kill everyone.

Facts

1. You only get fallout from a ground burst
2. The depositing of the dust-like fallout depends on the wind speed and direction as well as other weather conditions like snow or rain.
3. All radioactive fallout decays within a set time (I.E. The 7/10th Rule)
4. The human body can repair radiation damage providing the daily dose is not too large.
5. Distance, screening and time all help to reduce the effect of radiation.
6. Radiation exposure can be kept to below sickness levels by using a good shelter and by limiting the time of exposure to urgent tasks.

Fear

Because of the resultant fallout, so much of our food and water will be poisoned that people will starve and die even in fallout areas where there is sufficient food and water.

Fact

1. If the fallout particles do not become mixed up the parts of the food that is eaten, then no harm is done.
2. Food and water in sealed containers are not and cannot be contaminated by the radiation passing through the container.
3. By peeling fruits and vegetables it removes essentially all the fallout.
4. Even containing radioactive elements and compounds can be made safe for drinking by simply filtering it through earth filters.
5. Food contaminated (with the exception of milk) is not a significant problem in the immediate post attack period. Food and water should never be denied to hungry or thirsty people because of contamination.

Fear

Any person nursing causalities who are suffering from radiation sickness will become radioactive themselves.

Fact

Radiation is neither contagious nor infectious, but it does lower the patient's resistance to disease.

Civil Defence

Civil Defence in the UK is a complete joke right now; it is underfunded, if at all. It is on no one's agenda, local or national government and any volunteer civil defence resources have been eliminated in real terms.

However, during the Cold War, which began, some would say in 1945 with the Defeat of Germany and Japan and ended in 1991 in August with the end of the Soviet Union and therefore the end of the Cold War.

There was a complete civil defence system geared up for dealing with a nuclear attack it was called the United Kingdom Warning and Monitoring Organisation (UKWMO) which was disbanded in 1992.

Part of the UKWMO, in fact its field force, was the Royal Observer Corps who had a nuclear reporting role and operated from hundreds of nuclear proof underground bunkers roughly positioned between 10 and 15 miles apart across the UK again, they too were disbanded in 1992 as it was felt then that (for some reason) we no longer faced a nuclear threat?

I would suggest that as perhaps the threat of a nuclear war has reduced, however the actual threat from nuclear weapons delivered by terrorists or the threat of a nuclear accident has increased many folds.

In fact, I would probably suggest that in some form the cold war is still going on, as spying has increased since 1991 and hundreds more satellites have been launched to keep an eye on others.

So what of civil defence today, well patchy would be a good description to be honest? In my view non-existent would be nearer the truth I'm afraid.

Civil Defence Planning Today

Anyway, here are the official UK civil defence plans.

Following the end of the Cold war, Civil defence planning came to a grinding halt. It did so with a number of steps:

Back in 1991 councils were told to prepare for wider emergencies rather than just Cant. The Strategic defence review considered the level of likelihood in this occurring and we look at that elsewhere.

It remains, therefore, that the last piece of real, active Civil Defence planning as we know it is for the National Attack Warning system.ivil defence In 1993 the Civil Defence (General local authority functions) Regulations required councils to "make, keep under review and revise plans for their area and to carry out exercises based on such plans" for "civil defence purposes".

The Home office Emergency Planning Research Group was set up (1990) to look at some of the wider issues with Civil Defence including warning & monitoring (following the closure of the UKWMO in 1992)

"Dealing with Disaster" is produced by the Home office, giving advice for councils on how to prepare

The Civil Contingencies Act 2004 comes into force repealing 5 previous Civil Defence Acts and requiring various bodies to make plans where something "threatens serious damage to human welfare", affects the environment of the UK or "war, or terrorism, which threatens serious damage to the security of the United Kingdom."

The current state of Civil Defence planning is therefore very generalised but for those who have seen these changes happening will be clearly able to pick up continuations from the Cold War civil defence planning we have already seen. The Regional Emergency Committees have been replaced with Regional Resilience Forums who meet regularly and include members of the armed services, government agencies, emergency services and the councils.

Although the planning hasn't stopped it's just taken on a new perspective. For example the Emergency Planning Research Group had the following activities on its list:

Advice on the technical work involved with the National Attack warning system "the archiving of wartime civil defence related material" (Hansard)

The move away from the Cold war has seen the bunkers close, plans re-designated, organisations closed and - the end of the Cold war! Although war is in the portfolio of emergency planning today it is obviously not as important

The National Attack Warning System

The new National Attack Warning System (or NAWS) is a system developed in conjunction with the BBC and BT (along with other suppliers) to warn the nation in a time of war. It would warn of impending missile strike via TV, Radio and Phone (depending on your location).

The system was completed by 2003 (having started mid 90's) but most likely completed by 2000 and is now "maintained in a state of readiness during peacetime such that final additional stages of work can be quickly completed in a time of tension to bring it up to full operational readiness".

NAWS is primarily a system which enables a message to be broadcast even if the system has been sabotaged or damaged.

Key facts:

All technical & procedural work is now completed

The system costs "between" 200k-400k per year

When ready it can broadcast a message within 60 seconds

The public would be warned to listen to the TV and or Radio to receive the warning

Now (during peacetime) the BBC would broadcast using their normal broadcasting procedures and can transmit within 10 minutes when told to, or 30 minutes when not.

The system is capable of broadcasting after an attack

The system uses existing BBC transmitters - based "around existing transmission arrangements" but only "dedicated" transmitters within the network

BT would broadcast the warning message to remote ("certain") areas

A warning could be triggered by RAF High Wycombe - the "warning centre" which receives its inbound warning from Menwith Hill

The system "uses remotely controlled switching equipment" to connect to the transmitters

The information above comes from Hansard and not much further information exists in the public. Which transmitters are connected to the system or where the remote switches are, are top secrets and rightly so!

Wartime broadcasting service

The ability for the system to broadcast after an attack means that it has replaced the previous Wartime broadcasting service, based around the BBC at Wood Norton and regional broadcasts from the bunkers.

We know that the Pindar bunker in Whitehall has a broadcasting studio and the bunker still exists at Wood Norton so quite where/how post attack broadcasts would work is unclear. In effect, though, this one system covers 2 previous Cold War systems. Source http://www.civildefence.co.uk/

Today's Nuclear Bunkers

Following the end of the Cold war, the nationwide network of bunkers fell into disrepair and was sold off. The huge underground emergency War HQ at Corsham near Bath also got mothballed. Some of the bunkers entered active military service, whilst others were sold off privately. Local councils also have 'hardened control rooms' which mainly date back to the Cold War and Nuclear era. However, these now act as emergency control rooms, and are not referred to as nuclear bunkers.

RAF Boulmer

As part of the UK Air Surveillance and Control System (ASACS), 3 military bases were designated with ROTOR bunkers to continue radar operations. RAF Boulmer, Neatishead and Buchan formed part of the key line. However, today Buchan and Neatishead have been sold off with Boulmer originally intended to be sold as well. However, early in 2008 it was decided that Boulmer should stay operational whilst the previous Air control from Neatishead and Buchan was relocated to the RAF Scampton CRC (Control Reporting Centre).

The bunker at RAF Boulmer should not be confused with a Civil defence bunker for government purposes (of which there appear to be none in current active service), rather it is a military defence bunker. According to information from the

MOD the role of these (and the other military bunkers) would not change during a war and would be even more vital.

RAF High Wycombe

The RAF operations centre at High Wycombe, also has a nuclear bunker, costing approximately £83m to build. From this bunker the warning message would have been issued to the UKWMO and would be the trigger for today's National attack warning system.

HMS Northwood

HMS Northwood, the Permanent Joint Headquarters, which is situated in a leafy London suburb, also has a major and an active nuclear bunker. This centre has played a pivotal role in recent conflicts, and would be the key location for any wartime military response, operating from 100ft underground this nuclear Proof Bunker is staffed by the Combined Task Force 345 or CTF345 it is they who control the submarines that carry our nuclear deterrent.

"Each of our four Vanguard class or 'bomber' submarines carries Trident II D-5 missiles and is constantly on patrol, silent and undetected.

Every missile has a range of 7,000 miles and can deliver 12 warheads, each of which is eight times more powerful than the bomb used at Hiroshima. It is from here that the instruction to fire would be passed on to the submarine"

RAF Rudloe Manor

Corsham is/was home to a number of MOD sites, including the Basil Hill Barracks, Rudloe Manor, Copenacre and Hawthorn. Copenacre and Hawthorn were both based in stone quarries; Basil Hill and Rudloe Manor were both surface level centres.

As a result of a major redevelopment, Rudloe Manor (which closed in 2000) and Copenacre have both been sold by the MOD and relocated to Basil Hill for a MOD/PFI scheme called "Corsham New Environment". According to the MOD website:

"A major construction project to provide new facilities for the team that keep people across Defence connected is nearing completion. From satellite-phones used in Afghanistan, to telephones on desks in MOD Main Building, Defence Equipment and Support's Information Systems and Services (DE&S ISS) staff deliver communications systems right across Defence. Currently spread across a number of sites, the £690 million Corsham New Environment Programme will unite the team in one location at Basil Hill in Corsham, Wiltshire."

According to Alan Turnbull, the infamous Corsham Computer Centre – rumoured to be the new emergency government HQ is that "MASS Consultants manage the IT system within the underground computer centre in Corsham, on behalf of the MoD's Strategic Systems Integrated Project Team (StratSys IPT). It goes on to state that analysts who assess the performance and effectiveness of Trident use the IT facilities in the centre."

Some useful links

http://www.bbc.co.uk/wiltshire/underground_city/

http://www.secret-bases.co.uk/secret4.htm#burlington

MOD Bunker (Pindar bunker)

The MOD bunker in Whitehall (otherwise known as Pindar) become operational in 1992 and cost £126.3m to build. It is a "protected crisis management facility" which is the main communication point between Whitehall and the Permanent Joint Headquarters at Northwood.

The bunker comes equipped with a broadcasting studio and accommodation to house its inhabitants when working a 3 shift cycle. Those who would go into the bunker are "Ministers, senior military and civilian personnel, plus service and civilian operational and support staff" and is manned permanently.

Much of this information comes from a Hansard question and answer session available (Hansard info) and for photos inside the bunker you should visit David Moore's website.

According to David Moore's site it appears that the bunker is at least 2 layers deep.

This therefore appears to be today's main nuclear bunker which I had previously overlooked due to its use during recent wars. Apparently it costs over £7.3 million each year to run (based on 1994 figures).

From David Moore's website we know that the entrance to the bunker is sign posted "To Bomb Shelter Area" and that the bunker has a basement where diebuilding would provide an extra shield for the bunker below from radiation. sel generators generate the power.

An interesting note from Hansard is "A variety of routes exist which would enable the occupants to escape from the facility in the event that the building above it had collapsed."

Most likely these escape routes involve using the Q-Whitehall network, which has more details about the secret tunnels with which they should connect. What is interesting about the idea of building collapse is that if it collapsed, then the

So I hear you ask "What about me"? Where is my bunker then? The truth my friends is you don't have one for you and your family to go to. You are on your jack jones and if you do not learn to help yourself no one will rock up to help you.

Now you can see the need for this nuclear survival manual? The reason why I wrote it? You the citizen tax payer has been forgotten and ignored when it comes to your very survival, while the traitors in Whitehall who start wars just retreat to their purpose built nuclear shelters and hover around the bar waiting until it is safe for them to re-appear. That is disgusting and wrong, I say.

So what can we do to help ensure our survival in a nuclear situation? Firstly, I believe that a nuclear attack on the UK without warning to be very unlikely indeed. More likely I think would be a period of International tension, deterioration in international relations which could last weeks or even months. This would give us time to prepare if we had not already done so.

However, our emergency plans need to be able to be implemented within 7 days and their most vital parts within 48 hours.

Look, it is this simple, the Swiss and the Swedes have ploughed many, many millions into civil defence and into community and personal fallout shelters, BUT, if no warning comes all the planning is wasted, as your personal shelter with its minimum of 14 days food and water, etc. is totally useless to you and your family if you are out shopping in the big city when the bomb drops and you are miles from your shelter.

I say now that you and your family must plan to survive "in your own home" if you have nowhere else to go, stay put.

Radioactive fallout goes where the wind blows it. Even those living in rural areas will be exposed to the very same risks as those living in towns and cities. Nowhere in the UK will be safe from the direct effect of the weapons or the resultant fallout.

The following section on protection provides you with the information to help you and your family survive what would be the worst catastrophe in history. Such a catastrophe would be very difficult to comprehend, but even so it would be far from the end of human life on this planet. There will be survivors, learn and plan to be a survivor.

The first two things we can use to protect us from residual radiation are time, and the fact that nuclear radiation decays at a known and calculated rate. This means that the danger from residual radiation lessons with the passage of time. The decay rate, as it is known does not change and cannot be altered.

To calculate it we employ the 7/10th rule. The rule is very simple to understand, the intensity of radiation falls by a factor of 10 as the time multiplies by a factor of 7.

This means that in effect 2 days after the burst the radiation is reduced to one hundredth of what it was, (See Fig 9).

The 7/10th Rule

Fig.9

Time After burst	Time factor	Dose rate rph
1 Hour	1	100
7 hours	7	10
2 days	7x7	1
2 Weeks	7x7x7	0.1
14 Weeks	7x7x7x7	.01

Next I want to look at the "Protective Factor"

All buildings provide a certain protective factor, depending on their size, the thickness of their walls, floors and roof and on where in the building you are in relation to the outside walls. The bigger the building the bigger is its amount of protection. For example: if your house is in a terrace, then the building on either side of you will increase the "protective factor". When we use the protective factor we are in fact calculating the difference between the reduced radiation dose rate received by a person in a building, compared to that of a person standing in the open.

Some protective factor examples are a caravan with its windows blocked has a p/f of 1.9; a two storey modern house with the windows blocked has a P/F of 13 on the ground floor, and a two storey traditional terrace has a P/F of 120 with windows blocked and the basement in use. These factors have been calculated in relation to the types of building materials used, and their location.

A protective factor of 120, means that a person in that building would receive 120th of that of a person standing outside.

As I mentioned earlier nuclear radiation is reduced as it passes through any material, some materials are better than others but the thicker and denser the better. (see Fig.10) Using this table you can now not only give your home its own P/F but you can plan how to increase its P/F in the future. The thickness of materials shown in Fig.10, are known as the "Half value Thickness" That means that they are the thickness needed to reduce the radiation by half.

Half Value Thickness of Shielding Materials Against Residual Radiation

Fig.10

Material	Half Value Thickness in Inches
Lead	05.
Steel	0.7
Limonite Concrete	1.6
Asphalt	2.2
Concrete	2.2
Stone	2.2
Brick	2.8
Earth	3.5
Plaster	3.8
Wood	4.9
Water	8.9
Fertiliser (in Bulk)	6.5

Beet "	7.9
Grain "	7.9
Potatoes "	7.9
Silage "	7.9
Hay (bailed)	32.9
Straw "	65.8

In Fig.11 you can see how only 2.2 inches of concrete will reduce the dose, residual radiation = Fallout, to one half of its original value and that of 6.6 inches would reduce it to $1/8^{th}$.

Protection

Fig.11

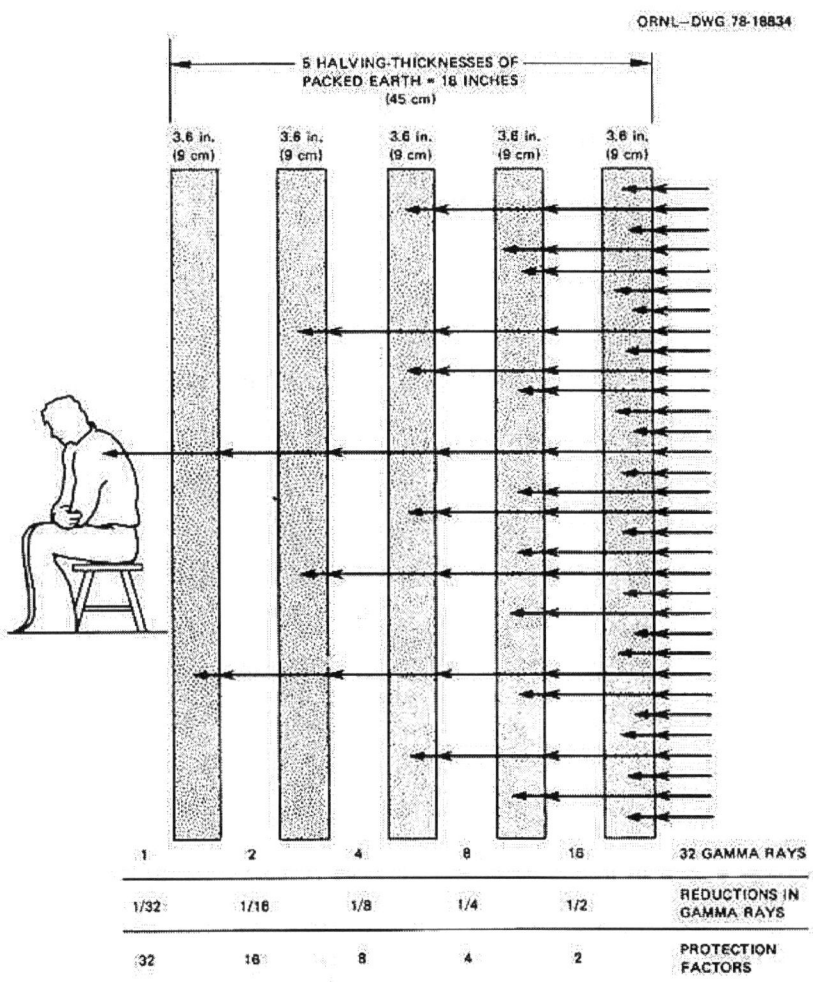

The same results will be achieved by 3.3 inches of soil, 2.8 inches of brick or 0.7 inches of steel.

Although I expect everything within the range of the initial effects of the explosion to be totally destroyed, even those outside this area will be at risk from heat, blast and fallout. Depending on the size of the weapon total damage could be up to 5 miles from GZ, with severe damage caused for even greater distances. Anyone alive one minute after the explosion has survived the initial effects and through proper preparation and planning can survive the residual effects.

Protection

Residual radiation in the form of radioactive fallout will present the greatest hazard to survival. Fallout is formed by debris being sucked up into the fireball becoming radioactive and falling back to earth. It can be carried by the wind for distances of hundreds of miles, before falling to the ground. The radiation from this dust is very dangerous as you cannot hear, see or smell it and to detect it you will need specialized equipment (A subject I will cover later).

If you are exposed to fallout it can cause sickness and death. If this dust alights on your home it will remain a danger to you and your family for many days after a nuclear detonation. Remember: As radiation passes through material its intensity is reduced so the thicker and denser the material the better.

Contrary to some opinion I say your best chance of survival is to stay at home. Do not head for the hills. As you know fallout is our biggest hazard to survival, as it goes where the wind blows it. Yes, even into "Nuclear Free Zones" and the more remote parts of the UK as well. So unless you intend to stay with friends or relatives or have a place to go 'STAY AT HOME' and plan to survive there.

The Fallout Room

You now need to select a room that will be your fallout room. Get to know your home and how it is constructed and give it a protective factor. Then make a ready plan to improve its P/F. For your fallout room, pick a room which is farthest away from the outer walls and the roof or which has the smallest amount of the outer wall.

Remember: Distance- the further you are away from radiation the better. Also remember 'Screening' your survival is increased by putting as much material as possible between you and the radiation.

Screening can be achieved by blocking windows and openings in your chosen room. If possible, make the outside walls thicker and don't forget the floor above you. Everyday materials can be used for this purpose, i.e. soil, sand, stone, cement, breeze blocks, bricks, water, furniture etc. (See Fig. 12 and 13)

Fallout Room and Inner Refuge

Fallout Room

Fig.12

These are typical weights per square foot of common building materials. When blocking external openings to increase the P/F of your home. Protective factors should be calculated on the assumption that the material used to block the openings has the same weight in pounds per square foot as the wall area.

Fig.13

Material	Weight
Brickwork	10LB
Stone	12LB
Reinforced Concrete	12LB
Asphalt	12LB
Hollow tile	8LB
Plaster	8LB
Boards	4LB
Tiles	14 – 18 LB
Slates	7LB
Cement Sheets	3.5LB
Corrugated Steel Sheets	2.3LB

Inner Refuge

Even though I have discussed improving the protective factor of your home, even greater protection is required, especially if radiation is at its highest.

I recommend building a lean-to shelter as an inner refuge the strongest angle for your lean-to is 60 degrees (See Fig 14) the inner refuge is where you should retreat to if a fallout warning is given or if you see the fallout yourself. Remember, it must be large enough to accommodate all occupants plus essential food, water and medical supplies, etc. For obvious reasons it must be as strong as possible and capable of providing equal protection to all, you will need at least one door for each intended occupant.

The Table shelter is the second type, although I wonder today how many still have an old Victorian type solid wood table high enough to get under and strong enough to take the weight of extra materials needed to improve the P/F.

If you are going to install your inner refuge under the stairs, then don't forget to pile extra material 'on' the stairs and bear in mind how many people will be able to get in with you and the stairs are on an outside wall. Strengthen this wall on the outside. Remember, even if your fallout room is your cellar.

The Inner Refuge

Fig.14

IF IT Happens

If the worst come to the worst and if the siren system is still usable you will need to know what the warning to the public mean. As with those used in WW11 the first and last have the same meaning as in 1939.

Sirens should be used to warn of "The Threat of Imminent Attack" the note will be rising and falling. These warning may even be given in an area which has no first-hand knowledge of a nuclear attack.

The All-Clear although given on a siren on a steady note- differs from 1939 as if may not be sounded until there is no further danger from fallout, which could be some time since an attack was carried out. The warning will last for one minute.

I am not sure that the siren system will work at all, in fact your only warning may come from TV and Radio broadcasts as part of the war time broadcast service.

Action at Attack Warning

If you are at home take the following steps.

1. Gather all your family in the fallout room
2. Shut windows and doors
3. Turn off gas, electricity, pilot lights, oil supplies
4. Put out fires close stoves
5. Draw curtains

If you are not at home

1. If within a few minutes of home, then return home
2. If at work or elsewhere and too far from home – take cover.

If you are outside

1. If too far from your home or other buildings use any cover you can find or lie face down in a ditch or depression and cover yourself with a coat or cloth etc.
2. Remember blast waves may take up to a minute to reach you. The light and heat will have reached you within 20 seconds.

3. As soon as possible after these initial effects, find shelter.

After an attack

The fallout will take some time to arrive and only if the wind is blowing your way. During this period the following actions should be carried out.

1. Check for fires, extinguish them with mains water
2. Check gas, electricity, pilot lights, fuel supplies, etc. are off "Do not smoke"
3. Do not flush toilets the cistern contains valuable drinking water. Replenish your water supply and turn off at the mains, turn off water heaters and boilers and all taps.
4. Repair any structural damage, cover windows, etc. to keep the weather out
5. Listen for fallout warnings.

Action at fallout Warnings

Remember: You may get a fallout warning without hearing an explosion. If outside, take cover, but before entering a building wipe any dust from your skin and clothing.

If in your fallout room: Now is the time to enter your inner refuge and stay there for at least 48 hours. If you have to leave your refuge for essential tasks or for the call of nature do so for as short a time as possible.

Although the risk from fallout after 48 hours is less, it is still dangerous and although it will be at a decaying rate the danger of 'new' fallout still exists. And without the specialised detection equipment you will not be aware of this. Listen to your radio; you will be told if it is safe to go out or not and if it is for how long. The longer you stay within your inner refuge the better your chance of survival.

Going Outside

Only venture outside for short periods. Use separate clothing and do not wear it within the Fallout room the same goes for footwear. If a death has occurred place the body in another room and label it. If no instructions are broadcast on what to next, then after 5 days bury it in a shallow marked grave.

Checklists

Nuclear Survival Checklist 'Before Attack'

1. Know the warning signs
2. Know what action to take at what warning
3. Select a fallout room
4. Block windows and opening in your fallout room
5. Improve the protective factor of your outside walls and the floor above you in your fallout room
6. Construct your inner refuge and provide it with a further protective factor.

Stock up and store in the fallout room the following

1. Enough water for each occupant for 14 days in sealed containers
2. Enough food for each occupant for 14 days in a cupboard or covered place
3. 2 radios and batteries for same, a mechanical clock and a calendar
4. 2 torches with spare bulbs and batteries
5. Candles and matches or camping lights etc.
6. Warm clothing, plus changes of clothing – hat, gloves etc.

7. Bedding
8. First aid kit, notebook and pens/pencils
9. Table and chairs, cutlery and crockery
10. Improvised toilet
11. Polythene bag/bin liners, strong disinfectant, toilet paper, plastic buckets and covers
12. Portable stove and fuel
13. Dustbins and lids, one for rubbish one for sanitation waste
14. Put extra water in your bath, basin, sink etc.
15. Paint your windows white
16. Place fire buckets on each floor
17. Remove all rubbish from upstairs and from around the house
18. Check your fire extinguisher is in working order
19. Take down your curtains and tape up your windows

Points to Remember

1. Fallout is most dangerous within the first 48 hours, so during this time you must stay within your inner refuge
2. Only leave your inner refuge for essential tasks and only then for the shortest time
3. The longer you stay under cover after a fallout warning, the better your chance of survival
4. Listen to your radio, take advice and act on it

5. Use water, food, battery power sparingly, it might have to last longer than you think. Water means life.
6. Use the same water for different purposes
7. Carry out your sanitation arrangements with care
8. Keep all containers closed
9. Keep rubbish and toilet water separate and covered
10. Remember hygiene – Keep Clean

Ventilation

This is of course very important, especially if your fallout room is going to be your basement or cellar.

Here is an example of the problems which face people using basements. In a basement 20ft x 10ft x 8ft there is a volume of 1600 cubic feet which is approx. 45300 litres

1. Of this air volume 20% will be oxygen = 9060 litres
2. Survival would be very difficult if say the oxygen level fell to 10%
3. Human beings at rest use about 250ml of oxygen per minute. Slow movement will use 780ml. When we use oxygen we replace it with carbon dioxide
4. Survival time for one person if lying down, resting, 350 hours – 14.5 days
5. Four people, however could only survive 3.5 days if there was no extra ventilation

This is before you start cooking and heating etc.

The problems associated with carbon dioxide

1. It is produced by badly adjusted flames or those burning without much oxygen
2. In small doses, it causes unconsciousness and death
3. But before this level is reached, effects such as a feeling of well-being and power is created

4. Judgement is impaired and mental fixation on small problems can result

I include this information as a warning. If sufficient funds are available there are commercially available ventilation/filtration units, but the price might preclude most of us.

Biological Effects of Nuclear Weapons

We live with radiation every day of our lives, from that given off by our luminous watches to x-rays at the hospital, to believe it or nor radiation from food stuffs. E.g. there is more radiation in a pound of Brazil nuts than in one of the reindeer shot in Lapland as a result of contamination by Chernobyl.

Now we accept these levels of background radiation, I mean a few Christmas's ago I sat down to watch the usual TV offerings on Christmas day, accompanied by a bottle of dark rum and a pound of Brazil nuts, none of which survived to see the end of Boxing day, needless to say having consumed one pound of Brazil nuts I felt none the worse.

Nuclear Radiation, however, presents a very much greater hazard because of its type and intensity and because it is designed to kill people within the target area or those down wind.

The primary effect of nuclear radiation is to release within the cells of the body electrical charges which interfere with vital functions of the cells and cause many secondary functional disorders as well as reducing resistance to infection and disease. The sensitivity of human cells to radiation varies throughout the body.

The most sensitive portions are those involved with the production of blood and the reproductive organs. The least sensitive parts are the muscles and perhaps surprisingly the brain. As any exposure to radiation causes damage to the body, it should be kept to a minimum.

For example, taking one sleeping pill will cause no harm, but if you took a bottle full at the same time you would fall asleep and possibly die. But if you spread this lethal dose over a month no harm would be done. Radiation works in the same way, a little radiation would cause no immediate effect.

In fact your body can counter up to 10r per day, but a large dose at once would kill you. But a large dose over a long period would produce no immediate noticeable effects See Fig.15)

Guide to Whole Body Exposure to Nuclear radiation

Fig. 15

Dose in r	Effects
Up to 150	No acute effects, but increasingly serious long term hazard
150 to 250	Nausea and vomiting within 24hrs. Some incapacitation after 2 days
250 to 350	Nausea and vomiting within 4hrs. Symptom free period 48hrs to 2 weeks, some mortality will occur in 2 to 4 weeks
350 to 600	Nausea and vomiting within 2hrs, heavy mortality certain within 2 to 4 weeks. Incapacitation prolonged for survivors
Over 600	Nausea and vomiting almost immediately mortality in 1 week

Health and Hygiene

In peace time, if we have a health problem we go to our own doctor or we go to the hospital. If we encounter a hygiene problem, we go to a public health officer, but where would we go in war time or when SHTF. Well after a nuclear attack the number of casualties would be too great for the doctors and the hospitals to cope with.

The problem is twofold: how many doctors and hospitals would survive and what or how long would current stocks of medical supplies last?

OUR very own survival could rest on how much medical knowledge we have and our medical supplies = first-aid.

Both the Red Cross and St. Johns Ambulance run local first aid courses I suggest that you take part in them as your life and that of your family could very well depend on it. The advantage to our fellow man or woman would be tremendous, imagine knowing what to do for the heart attack victim, the victim of the road accident or domestic medical emergency, we would be contributing to our communities and gaining respect as responsible citizens as well. (See their Role in War Fig.16)

So what medical problems might we face after a nuclear attack? Well to name but a few, everything from shock through missile injuries to severe burns. I don't propose to go into detail on how to treat particular injuries, I'll leave that for you to learn for yourselves, but I will cover the basics.

1. If a doctor or nurse or hospital is available use them if not You are in charge

2. Watch out for stoppage of breathing and serious bleeding. Remember 'keep them breathing – stop them bleeding'.
3. Watch out for shock and prevent it. Shock is caused by an emotional upset or painful injury or a massive loss of blood and is an acute circulatory failure. Prevent it and save lives.
4. Don't move your patient unless he is in mortal danger. Firstly, stop bleeding, maintain breathing, immobilise a broken limb.
5. Keep calm and reassure the patient, keep your patient lying down and warm, do not apply heat or make him sweat.
6. If unconscious never give liquids, this may cause choking to death or drowning if he can't swallow and remember no liquids must be given to a patient with an abdominal injury.

As I said, these are the basic rules, but there is no substitute for training and good qualification. A must for any first aid kit is a good first aid manual.

The Role of the British Red Cross Society and St. John's Ambulance Brigade

Fig.16

Phase	Role
Period of international Tension	(1) Community Training in Emergency Aid, Home Nursing and elementary Hygiene. (2) Mobilisation of Resources- membership and Materials
Conventional Warfare, Air raids etc.	Implementation of Aid to the Armed Forces
Nuclear Strike	All Stay Put in Shelter Conditions
Post-Nuclear Strike	Activate First Aid Posts
Survival Phase	Preservation of Health and Morale in the Community

The key to good health is good hygiene – important at home and work today but crucial post nuclear. However well-stocked our arsenal of bleaches, cleaning products, sprays, etc. we will run out, what then? A lot of good hygiene is good common sense, from food storage and handling to waste disposal. Food must be stored in dry, cool conditions, it must be sealed we must check it's eaten by date. It must be cooked properly to kill bacteria, once cooked it must be either eaten or preserved for later use.

Flies alone spread disease and their control would render a most valuable service the following are some basic rules.

1. Burial or burning of all refuse, especially kitchen waste
2. Protection of food especially cooked food
3. Proper disposal of sewage water, especially greasy water, from communal kitchens
4. Strict sanitation, hygiene
5. Doses of radiation large enough to kill a human being would not even sterilise insects. Kill all insects by whatever means: failure to do this would result in plagues of disease carrying insects swarming wherever humans or animals existed.
6. The provision of safe drinking water for all

Sanitation

Assume that your toilet will not flush; anyway the cistern contains a valuable source of water, so you will have to make other arrangements. To make a survival toilet I suggest two possible methods. The first is the easiest and consists of a bucket and a bin liner. The second is the deluxe type, by taking the seat out of a dining chair and placing it over the bucket you can sit and read this manual in comfort.

Your bucket should have a firm fitting cover when not in use and should be regularly doused with disinfectant to reduce smells and the risk to health. As each bin liner is filled, it should be sealed and placed as far away from the inner refuge as possible and placed in a dustbin with a firm fitting lid.

Don't forget a second dustbin for other rubbish also with a well-fitting lid.

Water

The elixir of life, try for only 24 hours to do without water and see how you feel. The average person needs to drink enough water per day so that they urinate at least one pint each day to flush the kidneys. In cool conditions a minimum of 2 pints per person per day must be drunk. Your emergency drinking water supply must be at least 2 pints per person per day x 14 day minimum. However, in my opinion you should have 1 gallon per person per day, and that is what I have.

To store this amount of water you can use everything from Jerry cans to your bath and sink etc. All tap water collected pre-attack will be safe but it must be kept covered. Fact: Gamma rays passing through water stored in a container will not make the water radioactive.

But remember to wash off any water container to remove any dust before opening it.

(N.B. Your hot water tank contains between 20 and 60 gallons: you can use the water in the pipes in your home. By turning off at the stopcock, and then by turning on the highest tap to allow air to enter, you can draw off water as needed from the lowest tap.

Water from rivers and streams is not safe to drink unless filtered and then boiled or chlorinated (normal service practice).

Purification

Waterborne diseases probably would kill more survivors of a nuclear attack than would radioactive contaminated water. For long time storage, all water must be disinfected. Since even a few organisms may multiply rapidly and give stored water a bad taste or smell, sodium hypochlorite is ideal for chlorination. This chemical is used in household bleach often marked on the bottle as its only active ingredient. Unfortunately, modern household bleaches now include colouring and thickening agents and a detergent making them unsuitable for purification of water.

Sodium Hypochlorite can still be obtained from wholesale stockists but it is unlikely that you will be able to buy it in quantities less than a 5 gallon container. A further problem is that this chemical only has a one year shelf life. Two other products to use are Milton and the normal water purification tablets (puritabs) these are calcium Hypochlorite and as long as they are kept dry in airtight containers have a long shelf life. Now Aquatabs are the "in" thing to use.

I recommend any of the following Purificup, Lifesaver bottle, OKO bottle and the Water-to-Go bottle all of which work without the need to boil water ever again.

Before disinfecting any water, especially from streams and ponds etc. If you do not have a water filtration bottle, it must be filtered (See Fig.17) If you use an earth/sand filter, then essentially all fallout particles will be removed. In heavily contaminated areas about 99% of the fallout in water could be removed by filtering out the particles through the ordinary earth. Note: earth filters are more effective in removing radioactive iodine's than are ordinary water softeners or charcoal filters.

Simple Soil Filter

Fig.17

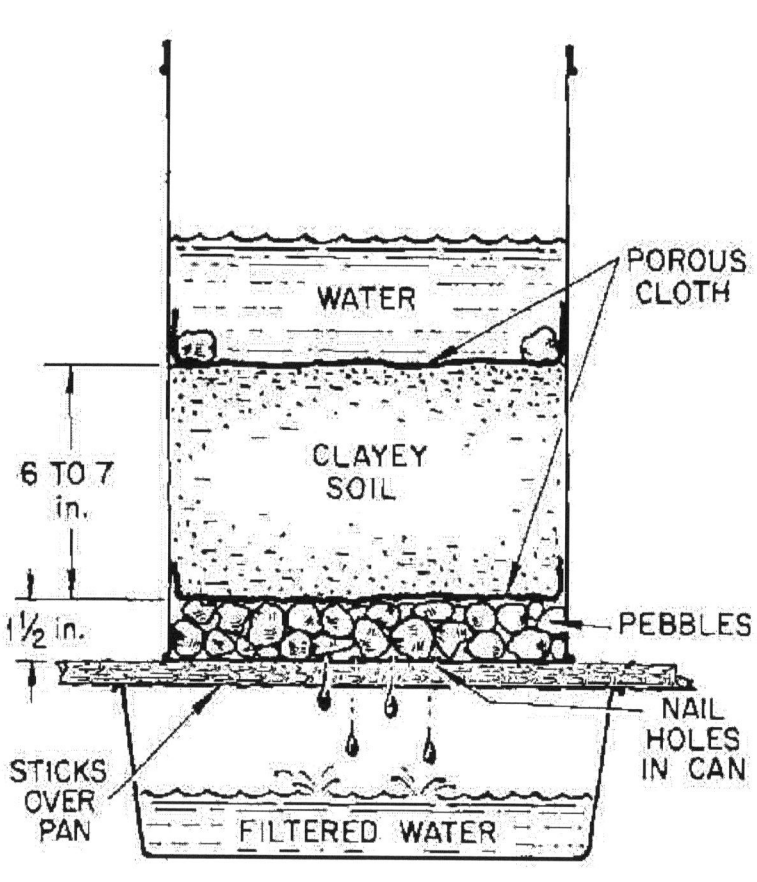

EXPEDIENT FILTRATION

Another method of purification is tincture of iodine used at a level of 2%. Add 5 drops to quart of clear water and let stand for 20 minutes, if the water is cloudy add 10 drops to each quart. Remember: purification does not remove all contamination caused by fallout particles. These methods of treating water must be learned if you are to survive (See Fig18).

Effects of Nuclear Strike on the Water Industry

Fig.18

Some destruction or damage to a few installations and distribution systems. However, these are considered to be less vulnerable than other Public Utilities such as Power Stations
Power failures Affecting Pumping Stations
Increased Local Demand Due to population Movement and People Stocking up their Water Stores
Possible Shortage of Control, Operating and Repair Staff
Contamination
Pollution Resulting from Sewage Infiltration

Improvised Storage of Water

You can store water in plastic lined boxes, alternatively dig a hole in the ground and place earth around the rim to stop rain water running into the hole. Line the hole with polythene sheet, fill with water and cover. If mains water is kept in this or other improvised storage containers and left to stand for more than 1 or 2 weeks it should be chlorinated before drinking. If in any doubt purify all water regardless of storage times.

Try this method: if water must be carted from A to B line sacks, trouser legs or pillow cases with larger diameter plastic bags. With a plastic lined water filled trouser leg or sack carried front and back over a person's shoulder 4 to 6 gallons (40 to 60 LB) of water can be carried for a considerable distance.

Earth Filter

To build your earth filter follow these simple instructions

1. Perforate the bottom of a 5 gallon can, a large bucket or similar container with about a dozen holes from the bottom upwards within about 2 inches from the centre.
2. Place a layer about 1½ inches thick of washed pebbles and small stones on the bottom. If you cannot find

pebbles of stones, use twisted coat hanger wires or small sticks.
3. Cover the pebbles with a large layer of terry cloth towel, sackcloth or similar, cut the cloth into a rough circular shape about 3 inches larger than the diameter of the container.
4. The cloth should be covered with 6 or 7 inches of top soil taken from at least 4 inches below the surface. First pulverise the soil, then gently press it in layers over the cloth so that the cloth is held close to the sides of the container.
5. Completely cover the surface of the soil with one thickness of porous fabric like a bath towel. This will keep the soil from being eroded as water is poured into the filter. The cloth will of course remove some of the particles from the water, by putting stones on the edges of the cloth it will stay in place.
6. The filter should be supported on rods or sticks placed across the top of a container that is larger than the filter.
7. Contaminated water which has been allowed to settle (See Settling) should be poured into the filter the filtered water should then be disinfected by one of the previously described methods.
8. If the earth used is sandy clay loam for example, your filter will produce 6 quarts of clean water per hour, however if the filtration rate is faster than about 1 quart in 10 minutes remove the upper fabric and recompress the soil. After several hours, the rate will reduce to about 2 quarts an hour. 1 quart is just under a litre.

9. If the filtration rate becomes too slow, it can be speeded up by removing and rinsing the surface fabric.
10. To increase the life of your filter, allow muddy water to settle as below and after 50 quarts have been filtered, rebuild your filter using fresh soil.

Settling

This is one of the easiest ways to remove radioactive particles from water and it also extends the life of your filter. To settle water, first fill a bucket or a container three-quarters full with contaminated water. Dig pulverised clay or clayey soil from 4 or more inches below ground and stir into the water. Stir until nearly all the clay particles are suspended in the water.

Let the clay settle for 6 hours. As the clay settles it will carry most of the suspended fallout particles to the bottom of the container and cover them. Now all you have to do is tip or siphon the clean water and disinfect it.

Settling and Filtering

Although the dissolved radioactive material usually is only a minor danger in the fallout contaminated water, it is safest to filter even the clearest water produced by settling then disinfect it.

I think that much about drinking water will be guess work but I believe that the statements in (Fig.19) are true although they may not all be applicable to you. For a recap on the method of water purification and sterilisation (See Fig.20)

Use the Following

Fig.19

Any Water in Preference to	No Water
Underground in Preference to	Surface water
Clean Water in Preference to	Dirty water
Dirty Water passed Through a Slow Sand filter in Preference to	UN-filtrated water
Chlorinated Dirty looking Water in Preference to	Clean looks UN-chlorinated
Chlorinated Clean Water in preference to	Dirty Looking Water

Remember:

Fig.20

To Sterilise Water, Boil it vigorously for at least one minute. If the water has not been filtered, it may be wiser to increase the boiling time to as long as 20 minutes. Or use a household bleach solution 5.25 per cent sodium hypochlorite.

If the water is clear add 8 drops of bleach to 5 litres of water. If the water is cloudy use 16 drops. Check after 30 minutes. If there is not a distinct taste or smell of chlorine, repeat the bleach treatment and let the water stand for another 15 minutes.

Other alternatives are iodine, Milton and water purification tablets

Don't forget: - Bleach has a limited shelf life

Reducing the risk of Fire

An important factor in your survival is to reduce the risk of fire in your home. You must remove paper and cardboard from upper floors where a fire is most likely. This must all bedding as well.

Remove net curtains, but leave heavy curtains and blinds as these when drawn give protection from flying glass. Paint your windows with whitewash or light white emulsion paint, to reflect away as much light and heat flash as possible. Close all doors in your home to help prevent the spread of fire. Remove any rubbish from around the outside of your home.

Put any fire blankets or fire extinguishers in the fallout room, Remember to show all your family members how to turn off electricity, gas, pilot light and oil fires and of course how to operate fire fighting equipment.

Because of the damage caused by EMP and the increased risk of fire, disconnect all aerials from home and car and protect sensitive equipment by use of a Faraday cage or similar.

Post Attack Food Supply

Our lives today are made easier by our extensive food production, processing and distribution system. We take for granted our doorstep pinta (here in the country anyway) and our local butcher and supermarket. A massive nuclear attack or even a "dirty Bomb" could eliminate this complicated system within hours.

The problems are threefold: Firstly, our usual transport routes could be denied to us, by debris blocking road and rail links, or by their total destruction, secondly, the inability of our farmers to protect and feed all their livestock, and thirdly, grazing animals may swallow vast amounts of radioactive fallout along with grass and they may drink contaminated water as well.

This would result in damage to their digestive tracts as well as any radiation burns they may suffer from radiation fallout particles.

However the humble chicken is more resistant to radiation than most livestock and therefore would provide a useful protein source. Hens that have fed on contaminated feed produce edible eggs, as the bulk of the hens ingested radioisotopes are secreted in the shell. The humble chicken offers four more distinct advantages.

1. Their housing provides some protection
2. Their feed is usually stored, therefore, not contaminated
3. The consumer can slaughter and dress their own
4. You do not need to refrigerate them as you can keep them alive until you need to eat

These benefits apply equally to most poultry. In general the survival of livestock will depend on the farmer's ability to protect, store and feed his animals, obviously those kept under cover with food and water will have a much greater chance of survival.

Living off the Land

As a Survivalist and Prepper 'living off the land' is what I do, it is what it is all about, and I know that I am not alone in what I do, shelter building, trapping snaring etc. However, our ability to venture out may be reduced by high levels of fallout, or the unwanted attentions of wandering bands of pre-attack thugs now post-attack looters intent on imposing their will and demands through the use of force.

Even in extensive areas where levels of fallout would not be high enough to kill human beings, many wild animals would die from swallowing large amounts of radioactive particles in their food and water as well as from the direct effects of fallout.

Only in areas where there is known to be no fallout, should we plan to hunt, fish or pick wild plants.

The truth of the matter is we must plan to survive at home. Very few of us will have anywhere else to go. Earlier I covered the elixir of life - water, now I want to cover human fuel - Food. Up and down the country people survive on low calorie diets, in an attempt to obtain their idea weight or shape.

Very little regard is given to vitamin intake, and anyway if something goes wrong the doctor is only a phone call away. In the main these people live in our 21st century modern convenience/appliance age and do very little physical work. However, in the post-attack phase, manpower will be the difference between survival and death.

So as a Survivalist and Prepper I will require high energy foods to keep me going (Fig.21) shows a very basic survival ration giving you 2500 calories and 100g protein per day. But as you can see it is very basic indeed, and as I have said not very interesting and has two disadvantages, firstly it requires cooking, which uses fuel and secondly to most people in the UK it would be a very strange diet indeed but in a survival situation I feel they would put up with it.

Perhaps looking at it will inspire you to start preparing now by buying the foods you really like and begin rotating as you build up your stores.

Basic Survival Ration for Multi-Year Storage

Fig.21

	Oz per day	Lbs for 30 day ration
Whole Wheat Kernel	16	30.0
Beans/Peas (dried)	5	9.4
Nonfat Milk powder	2	3.8
Vegetable	1	1.9
Sugar	2	3.8
Salt	1/3	.63
Total	26.1/3	49.5
Multivitamin Pills	1 Daily	30

Storage Times for Survival foods

The variety of foods available to us today are almost endless, our choice is governed for many reasons of taste, availability, ease of cooking, advertising, price and so on. Most of us shop in bulk on a regular basis and the day before our shopping trip the larder is nearly bare. If we are to survive Post-Attack this will not do.

The most important point when planning our food supply to survive is, how long will it last in storage? Below is a list that if followed will provide you with an interesting and varied diet.

Note: I am not a lover of 25 year shelf life foods as I think they taste like crap and cost far too much.

1. Wheat, powdered milk, honey/sugar/salt, if stored properly will last indefinitely
2. Canned meat (not pasteurised ham), figs, rice, will last three to five years
3. Dried fruit, vegetable oil, will last one to three years
4. Peanut butter, tomato juice, and citrus fruit juices, multi-vitamin pills, lentils, dried green peas, dry yeast, soya beans or soya based meat substitute, vegetable powders = will all require proper rotation

5. Paprika (which contains a concentrated form of vitamin C) bouillon cubes, onion flakes, dry soup mix, sesame seeds (high protein, calcium and vitamins B and E), alfalfa seed (to sprout for seeds) two to three years
6. Dry grated cheese, garlic, and gravy, meat-seasoning – for food flavouring, mushroom soup lasts one year.
7. Vanilla, almond flavouring, cinnamon, nutmeg, food colouring and rennet tablets, dried vegetables for flavour and variety lasts two to three years.
8. Gelatine, any canned fruit (except fruits like rhubarb and pineapple, dates and prunes, lasts eighteen months.
9. Vitamin B and C tablets plus iron tablets, lasts up to five years, but check the date on the container.
10. Biscuits, - wholemeal/digestive, crisp bread, see packaging.
11. Cereals – muesli as a meal or available in bar form, lasts one year
12. Spreads – marmite etc., but because of its high salt taste, you should increase the drinking water, it contains vitamin B, there's a best before date on it but it lasts forever, ...
13. Tinned meat and fish, they taste better that dried varieties and are more acceptable when considering rotation, lasts two to three years.
14. Ovaltine used as a meal substitute, see packaging.
15. Fruit juices, last twelve to eighteen months.
16. There are a tremendous variety of dried foods and meals e.g. Vesta, pot noodles, etc. But you must bear in mind though the extra demand on water.

Note: With all commercially available foods, check the dates on the packaging for eat by dates.

Storage Times for Tinned Foods

Although most tinned foods have a date on them it is only a suggested eat or sell by date. They will in fact last longer, but there could be changes to their contents. These changes are in colour, texture, aroma and flavour. Store tinned foods as any other foods, somewhere cool and dry and mark on the tin the purchase date and refer to the list in (Fig.22) for use by times.

Storage Times for Tinned Foods
Fig.22

Products Including evaporated Milk	One year
Cream and Milk Pudding	One year
Prunes	One year
Rhubarb	One year
Fruit Juice	One Year
New Potatoes	18 Months
Blackberries, Gooseberries, Plums, Blackcurrants	18 Months
Raspberries, Strawberries	18 months

Other fruits	Two years
Baked Beans	Two years
Pasta Products	Two years
Fish in Sauce	Two years
Ready Meals	Two years
Hot Meal products	Two years
Solid pack Meat Products	Five years
Fish in Oil	Five Years

Remember: never use blown cans or badly dented ones, especially if the dent is on the end or side seams. However, you can still use 'slightly' dented ones, another point to remember is that once you open a tin it is as perishable as its fresh equivalent.

The suggested two week food supply does not take into account special dietary needs. It is designed as a 'basic' menu, nothing special, but it will still provide you with enough calories, vitamins and protein to keep healthy and offers variety when planning your menu. Remember: stock up now, store well, label, date, rotate (See Fig.23)

This list is provided to show what can be done if cooking facilities are not available or if cooking water is not available

Fig.23

Canned Meat or fish	2000g (4.5lb)
Biscuits, Crackers Cereals	2750g (6lb)
Canned vegetables	1800g (4lb)
Margarine, Butter, Peanut Butter	500g (1lb)
Jam, Marmalade, Spread	500g (1lb)
Canned soups	6 Cans
Full Cream Evap. Milk or Dried milk	14x small cans or 2x300g (1/2lb)
Tea or Instant Coffee	250g (1/2)
Sugar	700g (3/4)
Boiled Sweets	45og (1lb)

1 Multi-Vitamin Tablet per day	
Canned fruit juice, squash, drinking Chocolate if room to store	

A 'modern' two week food supply

Here is an expensive commercially available 2 week deluxe survival product and food kit for 1 person/ 1 week for 2 people.

An amazing kit at an amazing price at only $248.49 "The advert says" **I do not think so.**

Product within this Survival Kit: Emergency Duffle Bag on Wheels:

1 Aqua Block Water:

Swiss Army Knife:

Compact Multi-Function Shovel:

Survival Whistle:

Emergency Ponchos:

Deluxe Hygiene Kits:

NIOSH N95 Dust Masks:

Hand and Body Warmers:

2 Person Tube Tent:

Deluxe First Aid Kit:

12 Hour Bright Stick:

30 Hour Emergency Candle:

6 packages of Pocket Tissue:

Dynamo Torch/Flashlight:

Deck of Playing Cards:

Water Proof Matches:

Waste Bags:

Paracord:

Duct Tape:

Note Pad:

Pencils and pens:

Mylar Sleeping Bags:

Leather Palm Work Gloves:

Bandage Kit:

Water Filtration Bottle:

Water Purification Tablets:

Portable Stove and Fuel:

Fork Knife and Spoon and cooking utensils:

Wise Emergency Food Supply:

44 Servings Stroganoff Creamy Chicken Pasta Cheesy Lasagna, Chicken Teriyaki, Chicken Ala King Southwest Bean and Rice Beef Teriyaki and Rice Multi-Grain Cereal Honey Glazed Granola Brown Sugar Oatmeal.

My suggested food supply items

I have compiled a list of the top food items and emergency supplies that you can buy at the supermarket. The list contains foods with a long shelf life, items that have multiple uses, and supplies that are great for bartering.

Survival Food that adds flavour & comfort:

Comfort foods can be a huge morale booster during a stressful survival situation, something that needs to be kept in mind when starting to stockpile food. These four things can be stored for over 10 years, and are a great way to add a little bit of flavour to your cooking. If stored properly they will probably last indefinitely.

Salt

Sugar – Brown or White

Raw Honey

Alcohol – Whiskey, Vodka, etc.

Base cooking ingredients with a long shelf life:

The following categories of food make up the foundation of most recipes, and are all things that store well.

Hard Grains:

Stored properly hard grains have a shelf life of around 10 – 12 years.

Buckwheat

Dry Corn

Hard Red Wheat

Soft White Wheat

Millet

Durum wheat

Spelt

Soft grains:

These soft grains will last around 8 years at 70 degrees, sealed without oxygen.

Barley

Oats

Quinoa

Rye

Beans:

Sealed and kept away from oxygen the following beans can last for around 8 – 10 years.

Pinto Beans

Kidney Beans

Lentils

Lima Beans

Garbanzo Beans

Mung Beans

Black Turtle Beans

Blackeye Beans

Flours and Mixes and Pastas: 5 – 8 years

All Purpose Flour

White Flour

Whole Wheat Flour

Cornmeal

Pasta

White Rice (up to 10 years)

Oils:

Coconut oil – Coconut oil has one of the longest shelf lives of any kind of oil. It can last for over 2 years and is a great item to add to your survival food supply list.

Survival Foods that are great during short-term disasters:

The following items are great for short-term emergencies, and will stay fresh for a long period of time. During most disasters you're going to want to have food that requires very little cooking, or be eaten without any preparation at all.

Make sure some of your stockpile includes these types of food.

Other good survival foods: 2 – 5 years of shelf life

Canned Tuna and other fish

Canned Meats

Canned Vegetables & Fruits

Peanut Butter

Coffee

Tea

Ramen Noodles – not the greatest food in the world, but they are very cheap so they made my survival food list.

Hard boiled sweets

Powdered milk

Dried herbs and spices

Items that can be used for more than cooking:

Apple Cider Vinegar – Cleaning, cooking, and has antibiotic properties

Baking Soda – Cleaning, cooking, etc.

Honey – Mentioned again for its antibiotic properties and wound healing.

Non-food items to stock up on at the supermarket:

Bic Lighters

Toilet Paper

Soaps, washing liquid, washing powder and cloths etc.

Bottled Water

Vitamins

Medicines

Bandages, first-aid kit

Peroxide

Lighter fluid

Tinned Supplies

Charcoal

Disaster Supplies Kit Checklist for Pets

Food and water for at least two weeks for each pet, food and water bowls and a manual can opener

Depending on the pet, litter and litter box or newspapers, paper towels, plastic trash bags, grooming items, and household bleach

Medications and medical records stored in a waterproof container, a first aid kit and a pet first aid book

You will need sturdy leads, harnesses and carriers to transport pets safely and to ensure that your pets cannot escape. A carrier should be large enough for the animal to stand comfortably, turn around, and lie down. Your pet may have to stay in the carrier for hours. Be sure to have a secure cage with no loose objects inside it to accommodate smaller pets. These may require blankets or towels for bedding and warmth and other special items

Pet toys and the pet's bed, if you can easily take it, to reduce stress

Current photos and descriptions of your pets to help others identify them in case you and your pets become separated, and to prove that they are yours

Information on feeding schedules, medical conditions, behaviour problems and the name and telephone number of your veterinarian in case you have to board your pets or place them in foster care.

Fallout Room Foods and Supplies Check List

People living in the remote parts of the UK or those prone to flooding or being cut off usually have a well-stocked larder. They have also put thought into alternative emergency lighting, heating and cooking. This, you, the survivor, must now start to do. Food stuffs can be stockpiled by placing essential items to one side on a weekly basis. This builds up supplies in an inexpensive way. Remember: eat by dates and always rotate your food 'buy one, use one' you really should start prepping now.

Food Survival check list

Even tinned foods need to be rotated so mark your tin tops with a felt marker with its use by date and store all items in a cool dry place.

Milk-tinned and powdered

Coffee, tea and other hot milk drinks

Sugar and saccharine

Syrup, treacle, honey, jam, marmalade

Marmite, Oxo, Bovril, gravy mixes

Soup- tinned, packets, instant if possible to save fuel

Oatmeal-to be stored in a tin or sealed jar, eat cooked or raw

Fruit-dried and tinned

Vegetables-tinned or freeze dried that do not require refrigeration

Rice-tinned or in sealed bags

Butter or Margarine in tubs or peanut butter in a jar

Meat-tinned-corned beef, stews, minced meat

Biscuits-in a sealed tin

Seasoning-sauces, salt, pepper, relishes in jars

Sweets-glucose, barley sugar, plain or milk chocolate

Baby food-tinned or in jars

Vitamin tablets

Pet food.

Try out self-heating meals too, they offer variety and provide good nutrition.

Water

For drinking only: 2 pints per person per day x14 days 3.5 gallon A family of 4 will need 1 gallon per day.

Remember: to store extra water for cooking, washing and for medical purposes, and don't forget to cover all containers.

Bedding and Changes of Clothing

Sleeping bags, blankets, quilts, pillows, camp beds and mattresses

Warm jumpers, woollen socks, anoraks and coats, trousers for both men and women, gloves, scarves and hats

Boots, willies, underwear, waterproof clothing. Remember: to have a change of clothing for everyone.

Toiletries

Soap, face cloth, toothbrush per person and paste, razor blades and shaving cream

Deodorants, towels,

Detergents, bleaches etc. plus rubber gloves

Mirror, brush, comb, nail brush, toilet paper

Disinfectants, washing powder

First Aid Kit

Dressings, triangular bandage, safety pins, splints, scissors, cotton wool, plasters, tweezers, aspirins, eye wash, calamine lotion, Dettol, TCP, or similar diarrhoea mixture

Special medications which you may be on e.g., insulin, blood pressure tablets, and antibiotics in fact all your meds for 100 day supply if possible. Remember Lice and flea powders and rodent poison.

Equipment

Toilet-pot, bucket, plastic bags, Elsan or camping toilet

Torch with spare batteries and bulbs

2 radios and spare batteries

Lighting- candles, matches, camping gas or paraffin lamp

Cooking- camping gas plus extra containers or a meths type cooker but remember ventilation

Bowls- washing

Clock-mechanical type

Buckets-water cans, basins

Mugs-plates, soup bowls, jugs, teapot, cake tins, and Tupperware type airtight containers

Vacuum flask- for drinks/food

Knives, forks, spoons, kitchen implements, can/bottle opener

2 bin liners with extra liners

Books-games, paper, pencils/pens

Table-if there is room plus chairs.

Communications

The most basic type of communication is your mobile phone, you could buy a CB radio or take your 2mtr band amateur radio licence. Remember: do not switch on or transmit from your set until at least 6 hours after the last known nuclear explosion. Also remember to disconnect your set from the aerial before an attack and protect it. A spare aerial and a coaxial cable and an emergency power supply will be needed.

Home Made Faraday Cage

In the event of an EMP strike or solar flare, all of your electronic devices are vulnerable to destruction. Both cause a dramatic fluctuation in the magnetic field of the Earth that, in turn, causes voltage surges and damaging currents. These surges will irrevocably destroy any modern electrical components they come in contact with. By creating a Faraday cage, you can protect priority devices from this threat.

In 1836, English scientist Michael Faraday conducted an experiment on electrostatic charges that resulted in the creation of the container that bears his name. He was not the first to experiment with this concept; his work was based on research performed by Benjamin Franklin nearly one hundred years earlier, in 1755.

A Faraday cage is an enclosure made of conductive material that blocks both static and non-static electrical fields. This protects devices from a weapons EMP strike, a solar flare event, or a lightning strike.

Many websites have complex instructions on how to build a Faraday cage. There are also expensive Faraday bags and boxes that can be purchased. They are "guaranteed" to protect your items from an EMP strike, but collecting on that guarantee could be rather difficult, given the circumstances that would cause the necessity for that protection.

There are many less complicated ways that you can improvise an EMP-proof container of your own for a far less expensive price. Although these homemade Faraday cages are perhaps not as stylish and elegant as the retail units, they should be just as effective. The following items can be pressed into device protection duty:

- An aluminium rubbish bin with a lid
- A metal filing cabinet
- A metal tool box
- A gutted microwave oven
- Tin canisters or ammo cans

Insulate items by lining the container in a non-conductive material, like cardboard. You can also make cardboard sleeves for your devices. It is vital that none of your electronics directly contact the metal of the container. It is important to add that your makeshift Faraday cages should be grounded in order to disperse the energy.

What should you store in your Faraday cage? Anything that you don't want to live without post-EMP and anything that you can charge in an alternate manner is a good candidate for residence within the container. Some items that you might want to prioritize for a place inside the cage are:

- Radios (shortwave or windup)
- DVD players
- Extra hard drives
- USB drives
- Batteries
- Flashlights
- Laptop and charger
- Solar device chargers
- IPods
- Walkie talkies
- Inverters and charge controllers for solar power system
- Small pieces of medical equipment

Don't forget digital watches

Some preppers question the necessity of a Faraday cage. They wonder, why protect items that must be plugged in if the entire electrical grid is down?

First of all, if the grid does come back up at some point, a person with devices that have been protected will be in the vast minority of people to possess a working unit. If the device has been unprotected, even with the return of electrical power at the flick of a switch, the item cannot be repaired and used in the future.

Secondly, if you have planned other sources of power (such as solar or wind power) then the items that you have protected can be used with those power sources. If this is the case, also be certain to protect the proper inverters or solar chargers to be used with the stored devices.

Entertainment

To relieve boredom whilst within your inner refuge make use of the usual household games such as cards or board games, or even good old eye-spy.

You are a Prepper, so let the power go out. You've got it under control. You have your water, your off-grid heating method and enough fuel to see you through until spring, your food that can easily be prepared without electricity, your candles and fully charged solar lanterns. You are prepared to survive SHTF for however long it takes.

Except.

The kids.

They are… DRIVING. YOU. INSANE.

In all of your preps, if it didn't occur to you to put aside some activities that don't require power or a lot of light, you may be in for a rough time when SHTF.

Your children, since they are safe, warm and fed, don't understand (or care) that you had to prepare in advance to keep them safe, warm and fed. All they care about is…

"I'm boooooooorrrrrrrreeeeeeeddddddddd."

Here are just a few quick and easy things that have nothing to do with entertainment and everything to do with general comfort.

Keep boredom at bay

Keep a box of off-grid entertainment supplies in an easy-to-access place. Make one up for the different members of the family and make these items things that the kids are not allowed to play with at any other time so that they are novel and interesting when the time comes to use them.

Include things like stationary supplies, notebooks, pens and pencils, sharpeners, colours or colouring pencils, markers, glue sticks, glitter, puzzles, activity books, games, stickers… make it a treasure trove!

Be sure you include all of the supplies needed for each activity because it's hard to find things when your home is only lit by candlelight.

Now some or all of these games should do the trick.

Shadow puppets

Books

Hide and Seek

Telling stories – kids are especially engaged with chain stories

Reading aloud

Card games

Battleship!

Board games

Flashlight hide and seek

Flashlight tag

Guess the shadow

Toys that do not need batteries, like dollhouses and kitchens, dinky cars, and floor

Make your house an obstacle course. A way to run around, roll over beds, etc. to get some energy out.

Card games

Colouring

Board games

Arts and crafts

Send them outside, safety and weather permitting

Imagination games like playing house, cops and robbers, don't step in the lava, camping in the wilderness

Put on a play

Play dress-up

Collect song books and have a sing-along in front of the fire

Play music together (piano, makeshift drums, harmonica, spoons, castanets, etc.)

Make puppets and put on a puppet show

Make "campfire food" in the fireplace – for example, roast marshmallows, toast and make bannock bread.

Get out those old photos and finally assemble them in scrapbooks

Play word games like Hangman
Play with building toys like blocks, or Lego

Nuclear Survival Check List

This section I have designed as a checklist covering pre, during and post attack. Its use it's intended as a guide, each item to be ticked off once completed. It should be rewritten on an A4 sheet used with a clipboard and covered with clear plastic and put with this manual in your bug-our bag. Should the unthinkable happen then it is to hand. Consider the DO's of survival the don'ts DON'T.

Before Attack

Know the warning signs and know what action to take for each warning

Have you selected your fallout room, have you blocked its windows and openings.

Have you improved the protective factor of your outside walls and the floor above your fallout room.

Have you made your inner refuge, have you improved its protective factor.

Have you stocked up on and put in your fallout room the following:

Enough water for each occupant for 14 days and sealed it.

Enough food for each occupant for 14 days and covered it.

A radio (2 if possible) plus spare batteries.

Warm clothes plus changes of clothes, bedding for all occupants, first aid kit, candles and matches, note paper pens and pencils, table and chairs

Have you made an improvised toilet with a seat?

Have you got polyethylene bag liners, strong disinfectant, toilet paper, buckets and covers?

Have you got a portable stove and fuel?

Have you got a mechanical clock and a calendar?

Have you got extra water in your bath and sink?

Have you got your dustbins with lids, one for rubbish and one for sanitation water?

Have you taken down the net curtains?

Have you painted the windows?

Have you got fire buckets on each floor?

Have you removed all rubbish from upstairs and around the house?

Have you got a fire extinguisher, is it in working order

At Attack

Have you sent your family to the fallout room?

Have you turned off the electricity, gas, pilot lights and oil supplies?

Have shut all doors and closed the curtains?

Have you filled the bath, sink and basin with extra water?

Have you disconnected all aerials in the house from their appliances and pushed in all telescopic ones?

After Attack

Have you checked that the electricity, gas, pilot lights and oil supplies are off?

Have you put out all small fires?

Have you restocked your water supplies?

Have you turned the water off?

Have you checked your survival kit?

Have you repaired any minor damage to keep the weather out?

Have you taped up the handle and removed the chain from the toilet?

Important

Fallout is most dangerous within the first 48 hours. During this time you must stay in your inner refuge. Only leave your refuge for essential tasks and only then for the shortest time. The longer you stay under cover after a fallout warning, the better your chance of survival.

Listen to your radio, take advice and act on it.

Use water, food, and battery power sparingly water means life, reuse it for different purposes.

Carry out your sanitation arrangements with care.

Keep all containers covered; keep rubbish and toilet waste separate keep clean.

Detection equipment

As I've said previously, the fact that you have survived the initial effects means that you must now deal with the residual radiation-fallout. If you can't see, smell or hear radiation, how do you know it is present and at what level. Well, you can use equipment which is designed to detect radiation. The equipment is tried and tested and is used by forces worldwide and yes, it is available to you, the guy in the street, for what I think is an affordable price.

One of the problems, however, is the amount of disinformation and what seems to be a total lack of knowledge that surrounds the subject. Most of this equipment would not pick up the very low levels of contamination that was presented by Chernobyl because it is only designed to register levels which present a real danger to the user.

I've even seen personal dosimeters on sale with no mention of the charging unit. A dosimeter with its charging unit is about as much use as an ashtray on a skateboard "don't buy one". It looks like the NBC or as is now CBRN survivor and Prepper is without the ability to buy ex-army clothing and kit, unlike in the 80's when I had 75 complete NBC suits in my stash along with an S10 and replacement filters too.

I have however managed to find the kit below at a very reasonable price indeed.

A Pen Type dosimeter

A pen-shaped measuring device to determine the dose of ionizing radiation, the discharge of a charged condenser is a measure of the dose received by the carrier of a dosimeter.

CDV-750 Charger & CDV- 742 Dosimeter, £27.00 inc. UK p&p

CDV-715 Survey Meter, £50.00 Inc. UK p&p

This equipment is available from:
http://www.anythingradioactive.com/index.htm

Now I feel the only clothing option in an NBC environment is the following or similar clothing at least of the same quality.

Just surfing around I have found a local supplier for heavy duty Oil Skins at very reasonable prices I think, he also sells Safety Rigger Style Wellingtons and heavy duty rubber gloves, everything I need to provide a barrier between me and any fallout particles, along with particulate gas masks too. OK, I suppose it's not quite one stop shopping as even I would mix and match what is out there on the net to suite my own needs.

But for very little money indeed I could kit myself out with waterproof and dust proof clothing that will not rip or tear easily and that can be decontaminated very easily with a normal hose pipe.

Remember: if working with your hands up wear your sleeves over your gloves and if hands down most of the time, say just walking around then have your sleeves over your gloves and don't forget the same principle with your footwear and trousers.

I know that many survivalists and Preppers swear by ex-army kit, and I have to agree that it is the very best out there, but unless you have a contact who is still serving, it seems that the kit is no longer available to the general public.

An S10 is useless without enough replacement filters, have you enough fullers earth, how many Noddy (NBC) suits do you have "Operational life 24 hours", How many will you need, how many people will you need them for? Etc.

It is time to become realistic if we are bugging-in, staying at home, then we will not require NBC suits anyway, and my oil skin alternative will suffice as it keeps radioactive particles from alighting on you and with a respirator it keeps you from breathing or ingesting the fallout either.

N.B.C. Clothing

Look, I have my reasons clear for not recommending ex-army NBC kit, but there will be those who as I have said swear by it so I have included this section in detail for them.

Nuclear, Biological and Chemical protection comes in the form of the NBC suit. I will cover all aspects of NBC equipment, but with this footnote. This equipment is specialised and not cheap. It does not provide you with protection from fallout, except that it prevents you from breathing and ingesting fallout particles.

It has more of a Biological and Chemical protection role and it is restricted to a shelf life of 5 years and if opened an operational life of 24 hours. This means that for 14 days you will need 14 suits, respirator filters, decontamination kits, etc. and that's for each member of the family if outside in the open in a known fallout affected area.

As I have said before a much better choice I would suggest would be to buy a good set of oilskin waterproofs, wellingtons, thick rubber gloves and an industrial face mask. As this will provide you with everything that the NBC suit does for much less outlay.

However, if you want to buy NBC equipment, then bear these points in mind, if you are buying it from a friend in the army, check its date and condition, as the packs should still be vacuum packed. Remember: the NBC suit is useless after 24 hours exposure to the air.

Don't buy a respirator without an adequate supply of filters, if when you buy filters they rattle when shaken they are US so leave well alone. Remember: if you wear glasses you will need the special frame insert that fits into the respirator into which your own optical requirement is fitted. You cannot wear glasses and maintain a perfect airtight seal. Neither is any more than four days beard growth advisable for the same reason.

UK NBC/CBRN Kit Supplier

I have become very frustrated indeed with the virtual lack of UK NBC/CBRN suppliers on the internet. It seems to me that when the cold war ended in 1991 the UK NBC suppliers stopped trading there and then.

I know that there are still surplus shops selling the odd S10, or an N.B.C. suit, but, look guys, we as preppers and survivalists need access to the whole NBC/CBRN kit in a one stop shop and at reasonable prices too.

I have said before that I do not promote the surplus trade in NBC kit because of the use by times that are almost reached and because of its lack of availability in real terms.

I have also recommended the use of heavy duty oil skins combined with rubber gloves and willies as they will do the same job providing there are good seals around the face mask, neck arms and legs.

Therefore, civilian kit should be considered.

I have come across a UK firm that does sell exactly what we need and at reasonable prices too. The company is called UK Survive (a UK prepare company) there website is: http://www.uksurvive.com

I know that they mainly supply their masks and suits to protect against "Bird Flu" and "Swine Flu"

But that means we have equipment to protect us against these two threats as well does it not? However, with the quality of their clothing and their masks they also supply NBC/CBRN kit as well.

Here is a typical NBC suite

This NBC suite is manufactured from Tyvek® "C" garments provide 100% particle protection and protection against blood, blood-borne pathogens and concentrated inorganic chemicals, even under pressure. Remember to hose down/wash off before re-entering your fallout room or inner refuge as this will remove any radioactive particles as well as other contaminants. Cost £19.00

Here is their top notch gas mask

Developed together with industrial users, the X-plore 5500 sets new standards when it comes to wearing comfort and safe and easy handling.

The new full face mask X-plore 5500 is the ideal solution for those who need more protection - the solution for overall respiratory and eye protection. Optimum tight fit thanks to the double sealing frame, a wide field of vision in all directions and excellent ergonomics are only a few highlights of this mask.

Two lateral, safe and easy to handle bayonet connections enable the use of the X-plore filter series.

Face seal

Double-layer face seal with triple sealing action provides reliable protection and a secure fit for various face types.

5-point harness

Quick and easy to don without hair entanglement.

Bayonet connection

For easy and secure filter attachment. Both filters are inserted in a top-down direction.

Lens

Excellent, wide field of vision Extreme chemical, thermal, and mechanical resistance.

Universal size

Perfect fit for all sizes, ease of storage and spare parts handling. Cost £149.00 filters cost £19.00

These gloves are manufactured from a unique Tri-polymer neoprene, Nitrile, latex blend these gloves offer the wearer excellent chemical resistance and protection against a wide range of acids and solvents. 400mm long for extra protection, beaded cuff, unflocked, diamond grip pattern surface provides excellent grip even in wet condition. Cost £8.00

A basic bird flu kit

5 x Valved FFP3 disposable respirators

2 pairs of non-direct vent goggles

1 x 350 ml bottle of hand sanitizer **NHS approved**

6 x pair's Latex powder free disposable gloves

1 Bio Suit

1 pair of overshoes

They actually supply complete NBC/CBRN packs as well.

Remember: once you have bought your mask, suit, gloves and boots that is it, you will then only need to replace your mask filters.

If you have any questions regarding their products or you need to know what you require to be safe in these environments then please contact their 24 hour sales team on 0844 357 0273 or help@uksurvive.com and they have assured me that they are there to help you. Please also mention where you got this information from.

References

1 Linden, Thomas W. The Complete Nuclear Survival Manual. S.W.S.T. June 1987 pp 6-9

2 Lindy, Linda. Atomic Bombings of Hiroshima. Web, Wednesday, May 25, 2011 http://bestin-4o.blogspot.co.uk/2011/05/atomic-bombings-of-hiroshima.html pp 10-11

3 Linden, Thomas W. The Complete Nuclear Survival Manual. S.W.S.T. June 1987

4 Film Threads "A nuclear attack on Sheffield" Web. 1984 https://www.youtube.com/watch?v=3NxkEDpl-40&t=24s

5 Film "The Day After" An attack on the USA. Web 1983 http://www.youtube.com/watch?v=r2B7sdLPMfc&playnext=1&list=PLfeoMaLoMTiP78MO4hrJPkYgLsCBJIAa4&feature=results_video

6 Film/Cartoon Civil defence training film "When the wind blows"]

https://www.youtube.com/watch?v=4-XPsbNlhj0

Kearny, Cresson H., Edward Teller, and Don Mann. *Nuclear war survival skills: lifesaving nuclear facts and self-help instructions.* NY, NY: Skyhorse Publishing, 2015.

This book was last revised in 2001 with an Addendum on Hormesis by Cresson Kearny. It is published on a non-profit, non-royalty basis by the *Oregon Institute of Science and Medicine* (a 501 [c] [3] public foundation). These low prices also are made possible by continuing donations to the *Oregon Institute of Science and Medicine* given specifically to help meet the cost of publication and wide distribution of this updated and enlarged edition.

Afterword

Throughout this manual I have tried to present the facts and knowledge that you, the reader will need to employ to help you and your family survive the effects of nuclear radiation from whatever source it comes.

These are the facts whether or not you choose to accept them or not is up to you

Personally, I do not believe that there is any situation that cannot be survived, all are the facts to produce the plans and most important of all you need "the WILL to survive" without this will and determination you have lost before you have started.

Even without plans or knowledge, there were survivors of the first nuclear war. From Hiroshima and Nagasaki there were survivors. I am not trying to simplify the effects of nuclear weapons, as I said before, a nuclear war, a terrorist dirty bomb attack or a nuclear accident would be the worst catastrophe in UK history.

But we will get nowhere buy burying our heads in the sand hoping that the nuclear threat will go away.

-Tom

BOOK TABLES

Fire Zone of Ground Burst Weapons in Miles

The Power of the Weapon

Fig.1

Visibility	20KT	100 KT	1/2MT	1MT	2MT	5MT	10MT	20MT
2 miles	To 3/4	To 1.1/2	2.1/2	To 3	2-4mls	To 5mls	To 5.1/2	6.1/2
8 miles	To 7/8th	To 1 3/4	To 3mls	To 4mls	2-5mls	To 7mls	To 9mls	10mls
32 miles	To 1 ml	To 2mls	To 3.1/2	To 5mls	To 6mls	To 9mls	To 12ml	To 15ml

Fire Zone of Air Burst Weapons in Miles

Power of the Weapon

Fig.2

Visibility	20KT	100KT	1/2MT	1MT	2MT	5MT	10MT	20MT
2 miles	To 1.1/4	2.1/4	To 4mls	To 5mls	To 7 mls	To 8.1/2	To 10 ml	To 12 ml
8 miles	To 1.3/8	2.1/2	To 5 mls	To 6.1/2	To 8 mls	To 12 ml	To 15 ml	To 17 ml
32 miles	To 1.5/8	To3 mls	To 6 mls	To 8 mls	To 11 ml	To 15 ml	To 20 ml	To 25 ml

Heat Wave- Thermal Radiation

Power of the Weapon

Fig.3

Effect on skin	20KT	100Kt	½ MT	1 MT	2 MT	5 MT	10 MT	20MT
Charring	1	2	4	5	6.3/4	9.1/4	12	16
blisters	1.1/2	1.1/4	4.3/4	6.1/4	8.1/4	12	16	20
Reddening	1.3/4	3.3/4	6.1/2	8.1/2	11	16	20	25

The range in miles at which people standing in the open will be affected by differing degrees of skin burns from round burst weapons of different power.

NB. With an air burst in clear conditions, the distance could be 50% greater.

Crater Size in Feet for a Ground Burst Weapon on Saturated Clay

Power of the Weapon

Fig.4

	20KT	100KT	1/2MT	1MT	2MT	5MT	10MT	20MT
Crater radius A	300	510	850	1100	1360	1700	2200	2800
Crater Lip radius A	600	1020	1700	2200	2720	3400	4400	5600
Crater Depth	40	55	80	100	120	150	180	210

(A) To get ranges (radii) in dry soil, divide by 1.7

(B) To get depths in dry soil divide by 0.7

(A) To get ranges (radii) in hard rock divide by 2

(B) **To get depths in hard rock divide by 0.9**

Blast Damage to Typical British House & Strees Blockage for Ground Burst Weapon in Miles

Power of the Weapon

Fig.5

	20KT	100KT	1/2MT	1MT	2MT	5MT	10MT	20MT
Damage ring A	3/8	¾	1.1/4	1.1/2	2	2.3/4	3.1/2	4.1/2
	houses totally destroyed streets impassable							
Damage ring B	5.5/5 th	1	1.3/4	2.1/4	3	4	5	6.1/2
Houses irreparably damaged, streets blocked, until cleared with mechanical aids								

Damage ring C	1.5/8 th	2.3/4	4.1/2	5.1/2	7	10	12	15.1/2
Houses irreparably damaged, streets blocked, until cleared with mechanical aids									
Damage ring D	2.1/2	4.1/4	7.1/4	9	12	16	20	25
houses lightly damaged, streets open but some glass and tile debris									

Distance in miles of the effect on people in the open exposed to initial Gamma radiation

Air burst or ground Burst

Power of the Weapon

Fig.6

	20KT	100KT	1/2MT	1MT	2MT	5MT	10MT	20MT
50% survival for 450r	3/4 mls	1 mls	1.1/4 mls	1.1/2 mls	1.3/4 mls	2 mls	2.1/4 mls	2.1/4 mls

The Complete Nuclear Survival Guide

NO appreciable risk of sickness 75r	1mls	1.1/4 mls	1.1/2 mls	1.3/4 mls	2mls	2.1/4 ml	2.1/2 ml	2.1/2 ml

Fall-out dust carried by winds over a wide area and can even be talcum powder size.

Fig.7

Continental Fallout can Affect the UK

Fig.8

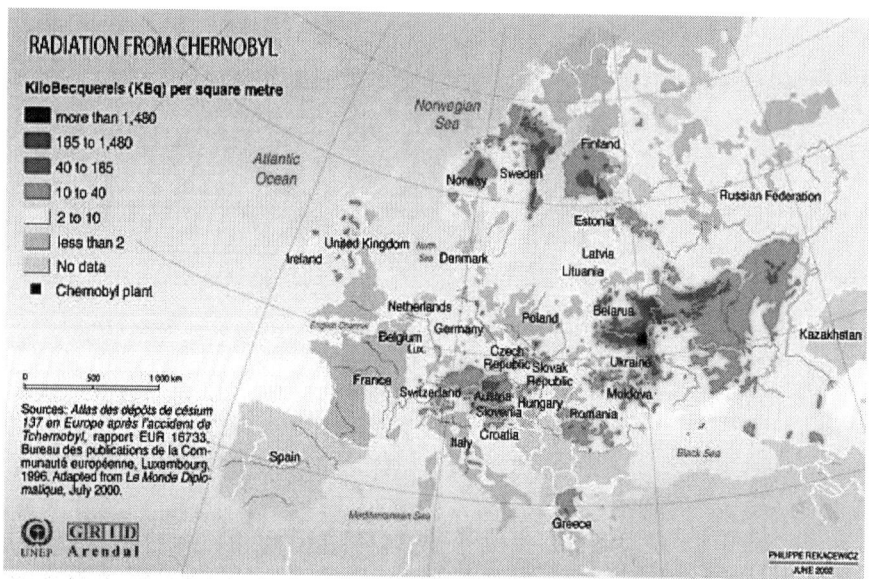

The 7/10th Rule

Fig.9

Time After burst	Time factor	Dose rate rph
1 Hour	1	100
7 Hours	7	10
2 Days	7x7	1
2 Weeks	7x7x7	0.1
14 Weeks	7x7x7x7	.01

Half Value Thickness of Shielding Materials Against Residual Radiation

Fig.10

MATERIAL	Half Value Thickness in Inches
Lead	05.
Steel	0.7
Limonite Concrete	1.6
Asphalt	2.2
Concrete	2.2
Stone	2.2
Brick	2.8
Sand	3.0
Earth	3.5

Plaster	3.8
Wood	4.8
Water	8.9
Fertiliser (in Bulk)	6.5
Beet "	7.9
Grain "	7.9
Potatoes "	7.9
Silage "	7.9
Hay (Bailed)	32.9
Straw "	65.8

Protection

Fig.11

The Complete Nuclear Survival Guide

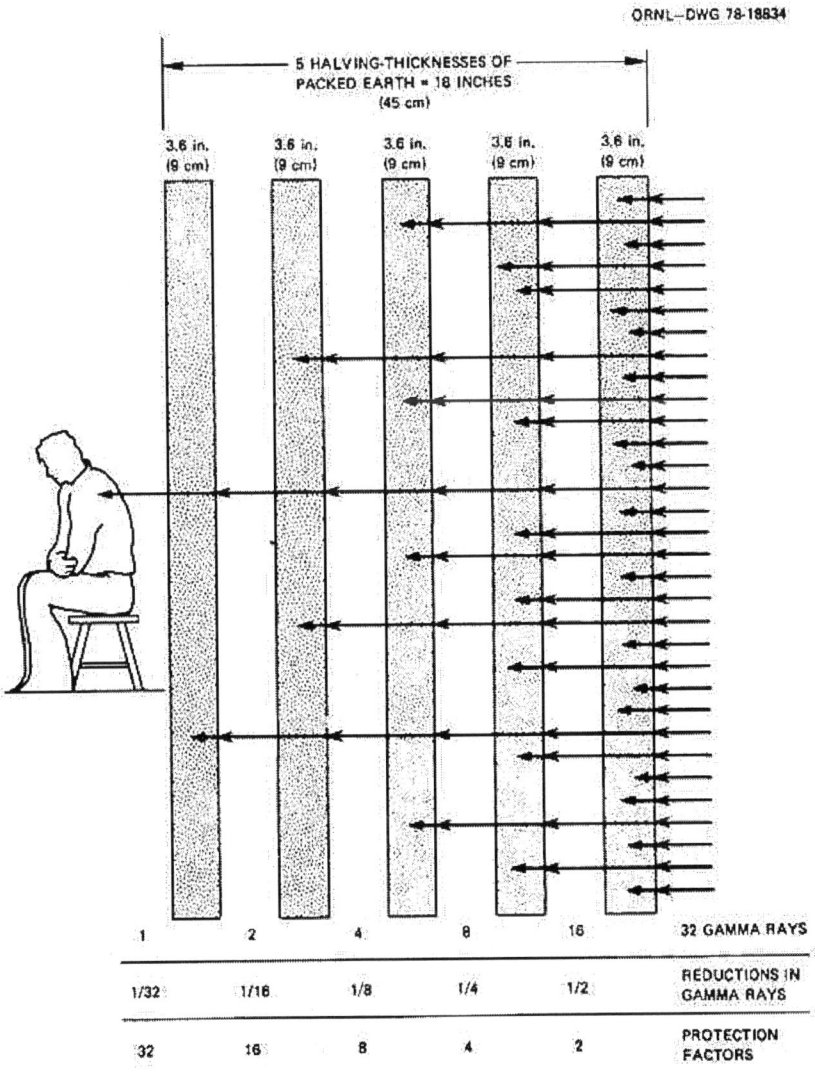

Fallout Room and Inner Refuge

Fig.12

These are typical weights per square foot of common building materials. When blocking external openings to increase the P/F of your home. Protective factors should be calculated on the assumption that the material used to block the openings has the same weight in pounds per square foot as the wall area.

Fig.13

Brickwork	Per Inch Thickness	10lb
Stone		12lb
Reinforced Concrete		12lb
Asphalt		12lb
Hollow Tile		8lb
Plaster		8lb
Boards		4lb
Tiles		14-18lb
Slates		7lb
Cement Sheets		3.5lb
Corrugated Steel Sheets		2.3lb

The Inner Refuge

Fig.14

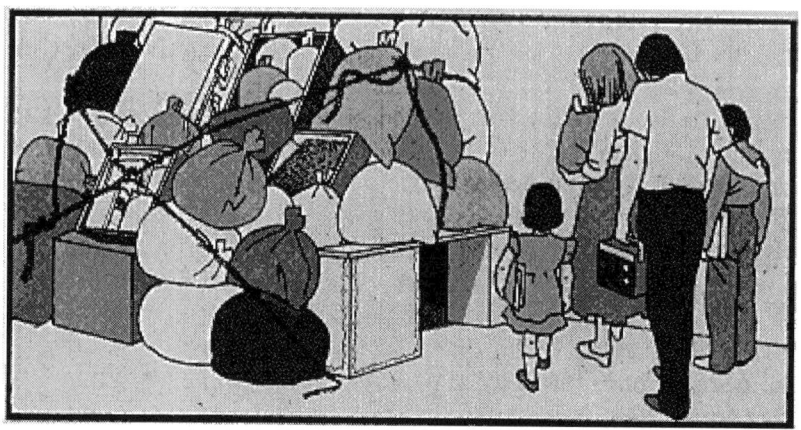

Guide to Whole Body Exposure to Nuclear radiation

Fig.15

Dose in r	EFFECTS
Up to 150	No acute effects, but increasingly serious long term hazard
150 to 250	Nausea and vomiting within 24hrs. Some incapacitation after 2 days
250 to 350	Nausea and vomiting within 4hrs. Symptom free period 48hrs to 2 weeks, some mortality will occur in 2 to 4 weeks
350 to 600	Nausea and vomiting within 2hrs, heavy mortality certain within 2 to 4 weeks. Incapacitation prolonged for survivors
Over 600	Nausea and vomiting almost immediately mortality in 1 week

The Role of the British Red Cross Society and St. John's Ambulance Brigade

Fig.16

Phase	Role
Period of international Tension	(1) Community Training in Emergency Aid, Home Nursing and elementary Hygiene. (2) Mobilisation of Resources- membership and Materials
Conventional Warfare, Air raids etc.	Implementation of Aid to the Armed Forces
Nuclear Strike	All Stay Put in Shelter Conditions
Post-Nuclear Strike	Activate First Aid Posts
Survival Phase	Preservation of Health and Morale in the Community

Simple Soil Filter

Fig.17

ORNL DWG 77-18431

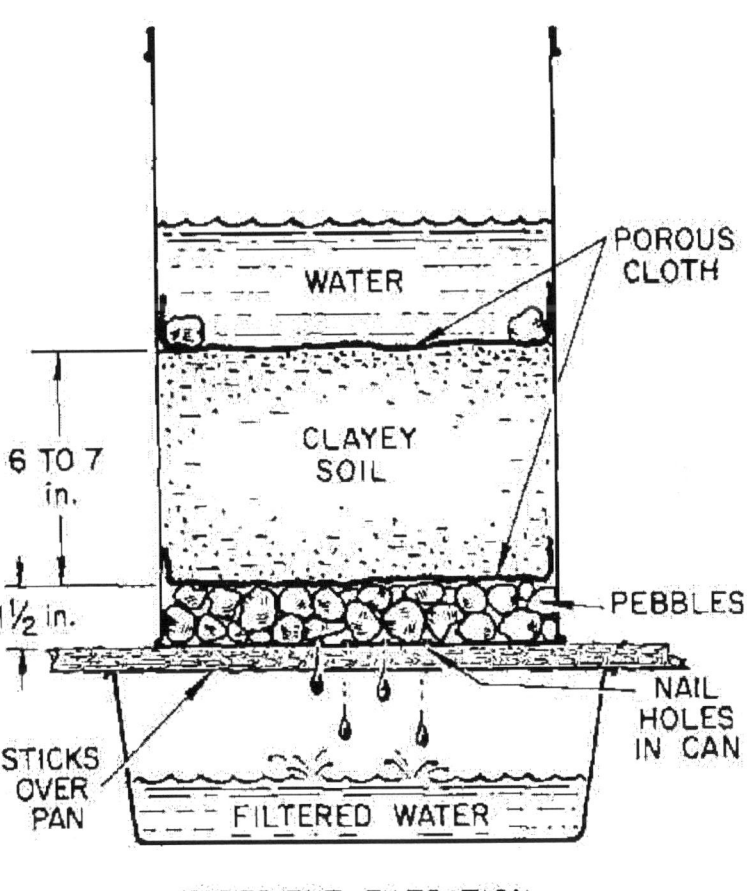

EXPEDIENT FILTRATION

Fig.18

Effects of Nuclear Strike on the Water Industry
Some destruction or damage to a few installations and distribution systems. However, these are considered to be less vulnerable than other Public Utilities such as Power Stations
Power failures Affecting Pumping Stations
Increased Local Demand Due to population Movement and People Stocking up their Water Stores
Possible Shortage of Control, Operating and Repair Staff
Contamination
Pollution Resulting from Sewage Infiltration

Use the Following

Fig.19

Any Water in Preference to	No Water
Underground in Preference to	Surface water
Clean Water in Preference to	Dirty water
Dirty Water passed Through a Slow Sand filter in Preference to	Un-filtrated water
Chlorinated Dirty looking Water in Preference to	Clean looking Un-chlorinated
Chlorinated Clean Water in preference to	Dirty Looking Water

Remember:

Fig.20

> **To Sterilise Water**, Boil it vigorously for at least one minute. If the water has not been filtered, it may be wiser to increase the boiling time to as long as 20 minutes. Or use a household bleach solution 5.25 per cent sodium hypochlorite.
>
> If the water is clear add 8 drops of bleach to 5 litres of water. If the water is cloudy use 16 drops. Check after 30 minutes. If there is not a distinct taste or smell of chlorine, repeat the bleach treatment and let the water stand for another 15 minutes.
>
> Other alternatives are iodine, Milton and water purification tablets
>
> Don't forget:- Bleach has a limited shelf life

Basic Survival Ration for Multi-Year Storage

Fig.21

	Oz per day	lbs for 30 day ration
Whole Wheat Kernel	16	30.0
Beans/Peas (dried)	5	9.4
Non-fat Milk powder	2	3.8
Vegetable	1	1.9
Sugar	2	3.8
Salt	1/3	.63
Total	26.1/3	49.5
Multi-vitamin pills	1 pill per day	30 pills

Storage Times for Tinned Foods

Fig.22

Milk products Including evaporated Milk	One year
Cream and Milk Pudding	One year
Prunes	One Year
Rhubarb	One year
Fruit Juice	One year
New Potatoes	18 Months
Blackberries, Gooseberries, Plums, Blackcurrants	18 Months
Raspberries, Strawberries	18 Months
Vegetables (apart from potatoes)	Two years
Other fruits	Two Years
Baked Beans	Two years
Pasta Products	Two years
Soups	Two Years
Fish in Sauce	Two Years
Ready Meals	Two years
Hot Meal products	Two years
Solid pack Meat Products	Five Years

Fish in Oil	Five years

This list is provided to show what can be done if cooking facilities are not available or if cooking water is not available

Fig.23

Canned Meat or fish	2000g (4.5lb)
Biscuits, Crackers Cereals	2750g (6lb)
Canned vegetables	1800g (4lb)
Margarine, Butter, Peanut Butter	500g (1lb)
Jam, Marmalade, Spread	500g (1lb)
Canned soups	6 Cans
Full Cream Evap. Milk or Dried milk	14x small cans or 2x300g (1/2lb)
Tea or Instant Coffee	250g (1/2)
Sugar	700g (3/4)
Boiled Sweets	45og (1lb)
1 Multi-Vitamin Tablet per day	
Canned fruit juice, squash, drinking Chocolate if room to store	

Printed in Poland
by Amazon Fulfillment
Poland Sp. z o.o., Wrocław